MACRO

M000234344

FELIPE LARRAIN B.

The MIT Press | Cambridge, Massachusetts | London, England

This book was set in Chaparral Pro by Toppan Best-set Premedia Limited. Printed and bound in the United States of America.

Library of Congress Cataloging-in-Publication Data

Names: Larraín B., Felipe, author.
Title: Macroeconomics / Felipe Larraín B.
Description: Cambridge, Massachusetts : The MIT Press, [2020] | Series: The MIT Press essential knowledge series | Includes bibliographical references and index.
Identifiers: LCCN 2019025844 | ISBN 9780262538572 (paperback)
Subjects: LCSH: Macroeconomics. | Globalization—Economic aspects.
Classification: LCC HB172.5 .L37 2020 | DDC 339—dc23
LC record available at https://lccn.loc.gov/2019025844

10 9 8 7 6 5 4 3 2 1

This book is dedicated to my parents, Vicente and Marta, who are no longer with me; and to my wife, Francisca, and our children, Felipe, Maria Francisca, Jose Tomas, Josefina, and Agustin, with deep gratitude for all their support and affection throughout my life. They are the true inspiration for my work.

CONTENTS

SERIES FOREWORD

The MIT Press Essential Knowledge series offers accessible, concise, beautifully produced pocket-size books on topics of current interest. Written by leading thinkers, the books in this series deliver expert overviews of subjects that range from the cultural and the historical to the scientific and the technical.

In today's era of instant information gratification, we have ready access to opinions, rationalizations, and superficial descriptions. Much harder to come by is the foundational knowledge that informs a principled understanding of the world. Essential Knowledge books fill that need. Synthesizing specialized subject matter for nonspecialists and engaging critical topics through fundamentals, each of these compact volumes offers readers a point of access to complex ideas.

Bruce Tidor
Professor of Biological Engineering and Computer Science
Massachusetts Institute of Technology

This book is intended for those who wish to know how the economy and globalization affect us all; those who wish to understand daily economic situations, as well as medium- and long-term economic trends; and those who are simply curious and wish to become familiar with a discipline that is not their own. More generally, it is intended for all who are short on time but long on interest to learn about the fascinating subject of macroeconomics. In short, it is addressed to everyone except my fellow professional economists.

My motivation for writing this book comes from a conviction formed through more than three decades of professional experience as an economics professor, government adviser, and policymaker in my country, Chile. I have a deep belief that every educated person should have a basic knowledge of macroeconomics, mainly because it helps us understand many phenomena that have important repercussions in our lives. The economic news often uses terms such as GDP (gross domestic product), unemployment, inflation, fiscal spending, and current account deficit. Without understanding the concepts behind these terms, one is clearly at a disadvantage in making informed decisions.

Economics is a fundamental component of everyday matters: people balance their expenditures when the general price level changes and affects their budget; they evaluate whether or not to acquire debt; and they look for work from time to time. All these decisions are heavily influenced not only by personal economic conditions but also by the overall economic environment.

The world has suffered dramatic consequences from bad macroeconomic management. The Great Depression of the 1930s and the subprime crisis of 2008–2009 are clear examples of the dramatic consequences of bad macroeconomic policies. The Great Depression of the 1930s was felt with devastating force in the United States, Great Britain, Germany, and the major economies of the time, with dramatic effects in the developing world, and prompted several economists to give macroeconomics the foundations of a modern science. The more recent subprime crisis also had dramatic effects, leading to a global recession, with millions of people falling into unemployment and poverty within only a few months.

Business leaders are much more sensitive to the economic environment since sales plans, investment programs, and wage negotiations are all affected by it. Moreover, the most successful business strategies are designed with a clear knowledge and understanding of the economy, in addition to some degree of personal instinct.

This book offers the tools to interpret what is happening in the local and global economy based on macroeconomic analysis. Those who would like greater depth and detail in the analysis may refer to the book *Macroeconomics in the Global Economy* that Jeffrey Sachs and I wrote in the early 1990s, now in its third edition.

Macroeconomics incorporates the most relevant economic events and phenomena of recent times. A substantial part of the analysis is devoted to the factors that explain the development of countries, so that the reader can understand why is it that while some countries grow, others remain stagnant. In addition, we look at recent economic crises, such as the subprime crisis and the subsequent euro crisis, addressing their causes and consequences. The last chapter introduces the reader to the exciting debate over globalization, its effects on the well-being of people, and how these effects relate to the recent protectionist dynamics seen in some developed countries.

So, regardless of the reason why you have decided to enter this fascinating field, you will find macroeconomic analysis has much to offer. I truly hope that I can convey my passion for economics through this book.

Because a book is the sum of many efforts, for which I am grateful and sincerely appreciative, I would like to thank Ana Isabel Farren and Oscar Perelló for efficient research assistance. I would also like to thank the staff of the MIT Press, in particular Emily Taber for her editorial help and suggestions in the preparation of this work.

WHAT IS MACROECONOMICS?

Macroeconomics studies the economy of a country or region from a broad perspective without considering too many details about a specific sector or business. Macroeconomists study changes in the aggregate, collecting data on the level of production, unemployment, inflation, consumption, investment, trade, and the current account, and other aspects of national and international economic life. Policymakers depend on macroeconomists' knowledge of the main elements and basic forces that govern each country's economy and the global economy when making decisions about taxes, industry regulations, trade policies, and more. These analyses affect decisions made by individuals and businesses, especially in a globalized world.

This branch of economics attempts to answer fundamental questions such as the following:

• *Why does a country become richer or poorer in a certain period?* For example, what explains the sustained high growth rates of the Asian tigers (Hong Kong, Singapore, South Korea, and Taiwan) between the early 1960s and the 1990s, and China's high growth rates after 1978? Why was South Korea poorer than the Latin American countries in the early 1960s yet today has three times the average Latin American income? Why has the Democratic Republic of Congo, one of the poorest countries in the world, had an average annual drop of more than 3 percent in its per capita income over the last thirty years?

• *What causes unemployment?* Why is there such a great difference among countries' unemployment rates? There is evidence for widely ranging unemployment rates even within the euro zone: 4.3 percent in Germany and 19.4 percent in Spain in 2016. Furthermore, what causes the unemployment rate to fluctuate greatly within a single country during a short period of time? In Brazil, for example, the rate was 12 percent in 2004; it fell to 7 percent in 2011 and returned to a double-digit rate of 11 percent in 2016.

• *What causes inflation?* Why are there such colossal differences in the rate of inflation among countries and through time? Moreover, several European countries experienced near zero (or even negative) inflation rates after the 2008 financial crisis, but Venezuela's inflation rate is higher than 1,000,000 percent, even though its neighbors in Latin America today have historically low inflation.

• *How can one country's economy affect the rest of the world?* How did the US subprime loan crisis manage to affect economic growth in East Asia?

• *What determines the value of one currency for converting it to another?* Why did the dollar lose value against the euro beginning in 2002 and particularly in 2009, then begin recovering from 2013 to today?

• *Why does economic activity fluctuate in the short term?* Why did Argentina's economic activity fall by almost 11 percent in 2002, grow by an average of 8.5 percent between 2003 and 2008, and then barely exceed an annual growth rate of 1 percent between 2009 and 2016? How do we explain the great moderation of fluctuations in the United States in the last half of the twentieth century? Why did so many countries in the world experience a recession between 2008 and 2009, and why has the recovery been so much faster for the United States than for euro-zone countries?

Before we can begin to answer these questions, we must understand how an economy is measured. Many of the key issues addressed by macroeconomics involve variables such as the overall level of production, unemployment, inflation, and the current account balance. We discuss these variables and how they are measured in the remaining sections of this chapter.

Production and Welfare

The most important measurement of an economy is the gross domestic product (GDP), a statistical indicator that tries to measure the total value of the goods and services produced within the geographic limits of a country or region during a specific period. It is calculated by aggregating the market values of all the final goods and services produced in an economy, that is, excluding intermediate inputs used in the production process (e.g., the value of roofing nails would be counted as part of the value of a new roof, not when the contractor or roofer buys the nails in order to start the project. An individual's purchase of roofing nails at a hardware store for personal use, however, would be counted directly in the GDP). Because the value of goods and services is determined by the prices paid by consumers and businesses, the GDP can also be understood as a measure of a given country's income over a particular period of time.

The United States contributes about 25 percent of world output, while the seven main developed economies (the United States, Japan, Germany, the UK, France, Italy, and Canada) together contribute around 49 percent (table 1). In this context, the Asian giants (China and India) have been gaining importance on the world stage: in 2017 they represented 19 percent of world GDP, whereas eight years ago they accounted for only 9 percent. On the other hand, Latin America and the Caribbean contribute 8 percent to global GDP.

Although all countries calculate their GDP annually, those with more statistical information calculate it

Table 1 Gross domestic product in the world and in some countries in 2017 (billions of US dollars)

Developed countries		Asian countries		Latin America	
United States	19,391	China	12,015	Brazil	2,055
Japan	4,872	India	2,611	Mexico	1,149
Germany	3,685	Korea	1,538	Argentina	638
United Kingdom	2,625	Indonesia	1,015	Colombia	309
France	2,584	Taiwan	579	Chile	277
Italy	1,938	Thailand	455	Peru	215
Canada	1,652	Hong Kong	342	Bolivia	37

World GDP: 74,581
Source: International Monetary Fund, *World Economic Outlook 2018.*

quarterly. Furthermore, some nations publish monthly activity indexes, which take into account most of the items that are used to calculate GDP and serve as a preliminary indicator of their likely quarterly figures.

Economists differentiate between two types of GDP: nominal and real. *Nominal GDP* measures the value of goods and services according to their current market price. *Real GDP* measures the physical volume of production for a given period using the prices of a base year.

Note that if the prices of all goods double but physical production remains constant, the measure of nominal GDP doubles, while real GDP remains the same. This is because price variations do not affect physical production.

Also note that although GDP growth may be positive over a long period, it may also show rises and falls over a shorter period. Such short-term fluctuations (expansions and contractions) in the economy are known as *business* or *economic cycles*. The moment of maximum output expansion within a cycle is referred to as its *peak*, while the lowest point is referred to as its *trough*. A complete economic cycle is measured from one trough to the next (figure 1).

When GDP is rising, the economy is said to be expanding, and when GDP is falling, the economy is said to be contracting. A *contraction* is signaled by the fall from a peak to a trough; an expansion is the rise from a trough to a peak.

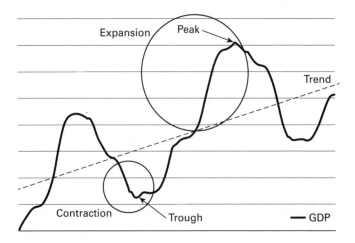

Figure 1 Business cycles represented by short-term fluctuations (peaks and troughs) in the GDP.

Economists often use per capita GDP (a country's total GDP divided by its number of inhabitants, expressed in a common currency such as the US dollar) to compare levels of development between countries as well as residents' quality of life. But are people living in rich countries happier than those living in low-income countries? To analyze the relationship between GDP and happiness, it is necessary to start by understanding what GDP is capable of measuring and what is left out of this indicator.

In a celebrated 1968 speech, Senator Robert Kennedy said that "the GDP measures everything except the things that are really worth living for." He was referring to the shortcomings of using GDP as a measure of well-being. For example, GDP does not measure "goods" such as free time or "bads" such as pollution. GDP has other limitations in its measurement, such as not considering the goods produced in the informal economy or within households. Therefore, economists have devoted time and effort to debugging GDP, seeking a measure more in line with the true well-being of people.

In addition, the reader might wonder how it is possible to use income to compare living standards between countries if with the same amount of dollars one can consume more goods in Haiti or Bolivia than in England or Switzerland, where the prices of goods and services are usually higher. Fortunately, this last aspect can be corrected by using a dollar adjusted by purchasing power parity (PPP) instead of using the current dollar. The PPP rate between two countries is the rate at which the currency of a country should be converted to ensure that a given amount of currency will be able to buy the same volume of goods and services in different countries. The latest (at the time this book went to press) PPP rates are derived from the 2011 report of the World Bank's International Comparisons Program and are then extended by different statistical providers backward and forward in time using the relative growth of GDP deflators.

For example, the per capita income in Mexico was US $9,304 in 2017, and Norway's was US $74,941. However, when we compare these figures in PPP terms for 2017, Mexico's per capita income rises to $19,903 international dollars while Norway's comes down to $71,831 international dollars. Although Norway's per capita income is greater than Mexico's in both cases, the difference between the figures is not as great when PPP is taken into account.

Economists are aware of these limitations, and in recent years, complementary measures that directly capture the subjective well-being or happiness of the population have been developed, such as the *World Happiness Index* and the *Human Development Index*.

Since 2012 the World Economic Forum has published the *World Happiness Report*, which presents yearly rankings of countries' happiness levels. The ranking is based on the results of a Gallup survey examining life satisfaction perceptions in more than 150 countries. It is interesting to analyze the degree of correlation between rankings of happiness and per capita GDP. For example, in the 2018 *World Happiness Report*, some of the richest countries, such as Norway and Switzerland, are ranked among the top ten happiest. Meanwhile, countries such as the Central African Republic, South Sudan, Burundi, and Yemen are not only among the ten unhappiest countries, they are also among the ten poorest countries.

It seems to be that, as the popular adage says, "Money does not buy happiness, but it sure helps." There is usually a positive relationship between the average income level and the levels of happiness reported by a country's residents. However, for some countries there are substantive differences between the two indicators, which tells us that other elements are also relevant for comparing the quality of life between countries.

Perhaps more interesting are cases of disparity, and here a comparison of Iceland and Costa Rica is instructive. Despite their very different cultures, climate, and income levels, they exhibit high levels of happiness. While Iceland ranks sixteenth in terms of GDP per capita and fourth in happiness, Costa Rica is eighty-first in the income ranking and thirteenth in terms of subjective well-being. This trend is repeated for other Latin American countries, such as Mexico, Chile, and Argentina, which show significantly higher happiness rankings than their income levels might suggest.

What can we explain these disparities? According to estimates from the *World Happiness Report 2018* itself, other variables, such as social cohesion, the existence of strong family networks, long (and healthy) life expectancy, freedom of choice, levels of generosity of the population, and perception of corruption, are also important determinants of how satisfied people are with their lives. Moreover, on average, for the entire sample of surveyed countries, 48 percent of the happiness score is explained by these nonmonetary factors.

The Human Development Index (HDI) also presents an alternative perspective on the development of a country, emphasizing that people and their capabilities should be the ultimate criteria for assessing the development of a country, and not economic growth alone. The HDI is a country-level measure composed of three subindexes reflecting the three areas of human achievements, health, knowledge, and standard of living: the life expectancy index, the education index, and the *gross national income* (GNI) per capita index. Each subindex captures one of the three dimensions through one or two indicators. The life expectancy index captures life expectancy at birth and covers the dimension of a "long and healthy life." The education index captures the expected years of schooling and the mean years of schooling and describes the "knowledge" dimension. Finally, the GNI per capita index, which indicates the average income in a country is included in the HDI index to capture the importance of having a "decent standard of living."

Unemployment

The *unemployment rate* is an indication of the proportion of people in the total workforce who are unemployed and actively looking for a job.

The short-run movements of the unemployment rate are related to fluctuations in the business cycle. Production reductions are associated with sudden increases in the unemployment rate, while increases in production are accompanied by gradual reductions in the unemployment rate. The unemployment rate is also related to flexibility in the labor market, or how easy it is to hire, fire, and retrain workers: more flexible labor markets are associated with more job creation.

Inflation

Inflation measures the percentage change in the general price level of an economy—how much more money is required to buy similar goods over time. The measure of inflation is the variation in the consumer price index, which is the average of prices of a basket of consumer goods and services. In general, countries aim to have a low and stable annual inflation rate, normally around 2–3 percent. Since price increases may actually be due to quality improvements or the omission of substitution effects in consumption (when consumers facing price increase change their usual consumption for cheaper options), inflation tends to be overestimated, which explains why the targeted inflation rate is usually higher than 0 percent Moreover, some economists argue that fixing a 0 percent inflation goal is too risky, since negative inflation rates (normally called *deflation*) are associated with adverse economic effects, and that a moderate rate of inflation facilitates the adjustment of consumer prices and wages.

Over time, the fluctuations in inflation raise important issues, which become even more complicated when inflation rates are compared internationally. As we will see further on in this book, high inflation rates often occur when a government needs to print more money to cover large budget deficits. If an economy suddenly has twice as many dollars as it did the day before, the value of one of those dollars goes down to 50 cents. We discuss this phenomenon in chapter 6.

Current Account Balance

The *current account balance* measures the exports of goods and services from one country to the rest of the world, minus its imports of goods and services from the rest of the world, plus the transfers that the country receives from abroad (e.g., foreign aid and money sent by citizens working outside the country).

In general terms, when a country exports more than it imports, there is a surplus in the current account. On the other hand, when it imports more than it exports, the country has a current account deficit. The concept of current account is closely linked to that of trade balance, as we explain in chapter 9.

Why is the current account balance so important, and what determines its short- and long-term movements? Imbalances are closely related to financial flows between countries. In general terms, when a country imports more goods and services from the rest of the world than it exports, residents of that country must pay for such imports, either by borrowing from other countries or by reducing their holdings of foreign assets—dollars, for example. On the other hand, when exports exceed imports, the country's residents are generally lending to the rest of the world. Therefore, our study of current account imbalances is closely associated with the study of why a country's residents lend money to the rest of the world or why they borrow from the rest of the world.

In the 1960s and 1970s, the United States had a current account surplus. However, over the next three decades the situation changed radically: not only did the country begin having current account deficits, but these deficits were the largest in the world. In other words, the United States was importing more than it was exporting, and more than any other country in the world. Indeed, in 2006 this negative balance was around US $807 billion, equivalent to 5.8 percent of US GDP and 1.4 percent of world GDP. Despite the strength of the US economy, some economists have issued warnings about this, since such a deficit seems unsustainable and an adjustment would be inevitable.

Economists were concerned for the United States because in 2006, the country was borrowing at a rate of more than $2 billion a day, which was probably unsustainable. Much of this deficit was being financed by Asian countries, especially China, which in 2007 had a surplus of no less than 9.8 percent of GDP. With the *recession* that began in December 2007 in the United States, part of this imbalance was corrected through a drastic reduction of imports, allowing a reduction of the current account deficit from its peak of 6 percent of GDP in 2006 to less than 2.4 percent in 2016.

A few years ago, the current account deficit became crucial for some developing countries, which became so heavily indebted to the outside world that they were unable to repay the loans and then fell into moratorium (which is the inability to comply with debt obligations), with serious economic consequences. A recent and painful example of this was Argentina during 2001 and 2002, whose situation will be dealt with in more detail later in this book. However, in more recent years, Latin American countries have sharply reduced their deficits, and several economies in the region have even achieved a current account surplus.

Macroeconomics and Globalization

Macroeconomic analysis has changed over time. After profound changes in the world with the fall of the Soviet Union in 1989 and the gradual integration of countries into the world economy, especially China and India, the economy has become truly globalized for the first time in history. Since many goods are produced using inputs from different countries, this process has led to a sharp increase in international trade, higher capital flows financing foreign investments, and the internationalization of production. What is certain is that the events of the international economy are increasingly affecting national economies, as evidenced by the international financial crisis that started in 2008–2009. This process has gained momentum, so economic analysis must consider interactions with the rest of the world. Even the US economy, the largest and most important in the world, is affected by what happens in other countries, and, of course, the rest of the world is affected by US economic trends.

Several countries in the world are experiencing sustained growth processes, which has reduced the global preeminence of the industrialized economies of North America and Europe. This situation has forced economists to pay more attention to what happens in other economies and has highlighted the need for deeper and more careful analysis. Ultimately, macroeconomic developments in

Ultimately, the implementation of sound and responsible macroeconomic policies, as well as knowing how to interpret and use macroeconomic signals, can make a crucial difference in the quality of life of the inhabitants of any nation.

different parts of the globe will increasingly affect people's lives in other parts, which translates into a greater need for understanding the forces of macroeconomics in a globalized context.

The effects of globalization on businesses and individuals are profound. Therefore, a crisis that was initially limited to the United States real estate sector quickly moved to its financial sector and then, through international ties, to other industrialized economies, finally becoming a global problem. As the recession unfolded in many countries, not only did important international banks fail, but many other companies in disparate sectors were ruined. Millions of people in the United States lost their jobs, with even more significant job losses occurring in the rest of the world.

Ultimately, the implementation of sound and responsible macroeconomic policies, as well as knowing how to interpret and use macroeconomic signals, can make a crucial difference in the quality of life of the inhabitants of any nation. This book explains why these policies and signals matter and how they work.

PRODUCTION AND EMPLOYMENT

In this chapter, we first analyze the main aspects that link economic activity with employment, then present the most important characteristics of employment and the unemployment rate.

There is a close relationship between GDP growth and employment: job creation falls in recessions—sometimes even below zero, meaning more jobs disappear than are created—while employment grows in times of economic expansion. This is not the case with respect to the relationship between GDP growth and the unemployment rate, which measures the proportion of people who are unemployed relative to the total *labor force* (i.e., those who are willing to work and able to do so). Recessions generate a rapid and significant increase in unemployment, whereas expansions tend to decrease the unemployment rate gradually. It is instructive to look at the latest financial crisis in the United States: the unemployment rate increased drastically together with a contraction of GDP in 2008, and, despite the strong measures taken by the Fed (Federal Reserve, the central bank of the United States, created to provide a stable banking system for the United States) to stimulate the economy, it took around five years to return to its initial level. A similar case was observed in Chile after the 1999 recession: unemployment began to fall only after 2005. It is partly because of these persistent effects on unemployment that economists are often so emphatic about the social costs of recessions. These facts seem to reveal the wisdom in the popular saying "It is easier to destroy than to build"—applied, in this case, to the creation and destruction of employment.

The Relationship between Production and Employment

The *production function* is the level of production that a company (or group of companies) achieves with given levels of available capital, labor, and technology. The capital of a company is formed by the plant, the equipment, and the quantity of primary, semiprocessed, and finished goods owned by the company (called stocks or inventories). The labor component is related to the total number of employees and the number of hours they work, and technology is the way capital and labor are combined in the production process.

When we study the short term (a period of one year or less), it is possible to assume that the capital stock and the level of technological knowledge of the economy are fixed. Therefore, large output fluctuations typically reflect changes in labor inputs and changes in transitory factors, such as strikes, civil unrest, or other shocks to production. Over longer periods, variations in production also reflect changes in the capital stock and technology.

The production function has two important characteristics. First, an increase in the amount of any input—capital, labor, or technology—increases production. The term *marginal productivity* is used to measure the increase in production that results from increasing any input by a single unit and is almost always positive. Second, the marginal productivity of each factor decreases when more of that factor is used and the other factors are fixed.

Let's consider, for example, an automobile assembly plant. Suppose a machine can normally be used by ten workers, although only five workers are available to operate each machine. Under these conditions, if an additional worker is hired, production will increase substantially. However, if more workers are hired without an increase in the number of machines, the increase in total production generated by each new worker will decline. If ten workers are needed to oversee the operation of a single machine, the eleventh worker hired will add little or almost nothing to total production. The production function and marginal productivity are represented graphically in figure 2.

How many workers should a company hire? Suppose that the company receives a price for its output and hires labor according to market wages. Its objective is to maximize profits, that is, income minus production costs, which in this case are simply wages and some costs associated with capital (the latter are considered fixed in the short term and therefore would need to be paid regardless of the number of workers hired). Hence the company's income is total production multiplied by the price of output, and the company must choose the level of labor that maximizes its profits.

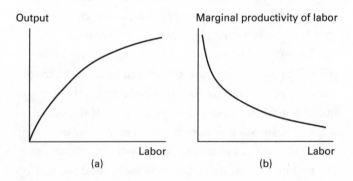

Figure 2   The production function and marginal productivity.

Now we will use the numerical example in table 2. If the wage is $20 per hour of work and the price per unit of output is $1, how many workers should the company hire? The table shows that the number of workers that maximizes profits is eight. Hiring past the eighth employee would reduce profits. What is special about the eighth worker? Note that this worker's marginal productivity is $20.2 and the extra cost in production of adding an eighth worker is $20. As a result, the eighth worker "pays for himself," as earnings increase by $0.2 once an eighth unit of labor is hired.

The marginal productivity of labor corresponds to the variation in production that occurs by adding an extra worker. Therefore, when labor is 3, marginal productivity is equal to 26.6, which corresponds to 101.3 (production with three workers) minus 74.8 (production with two workers).

The *nominal wage* is the pay of a worker expressed in monetary units of the current year, and the *real wage* is the nominal wage divided by the price of output. A profit-maximizing enterprise hires workers until the marginal productivity of labor is equal to the real wage. At that point, the contribution of the last worker hired to production is equal to the cost that this worker adds to the entire production cost. In other words, if the marginal productivity of labor is higher than the real wage, the enterprise will benefit from hiring extra workers, which means that

Table 2 An example of profit maximization

Labor	Production	Income	Marginal productivity	Labor cost	Profit
(1)	(2)	(3)	(4)	(5)	(6)
		= $1 × (2)		= $20 × (1)	= (3) − (5)
1	44.5	44.5	44.5	20	24.5
2	74.8	74.8	30.3	40	34.8
3	101.3	101.3	26.6	60	41.3
4	125.7	125.7	24.4	80	45.7
5	148.7	148.7	22.9	100	48.7
6	170,4	170.4	21.8	120	50.4
7	191.3	191.3	20.9	140	51.3
8	211.5	211.5	20.2	160	51.5
9	231.0	231.0	19.5	180	51.0
10	250.0	250.0	19.0	200	50.0

the current number of workers is not yet optimal. On the other hand, if the marginal productivity of labor is lower than the real wage, there are workers whose contribution is less than their salary, which implies the employer has hired beyond the optimal level. This establishes a very important general principle necessary to obtain the *demand for labor*: the higher the real wage, the lower the quantity of labor demanded, assuming a fixed stock of capital and technology.

Labor Supply and Equilibrium in the Labor Market

The next step in understanding how employment and output are determined in the economy is to define the amount of work that families are willing to offer to businesses. This starts with a simple decision of *work supply*, whereby a person must choose between working or enjoying leisure time. A day has only twenty-four hours, so each additional hour dedicated to work is one hour less available for leisure. Leisure is understood as recreational activities, such as reading for pleasure, listening to music, playing sports, going to the theater, or even sleeping. However, the economic measurement of leisure is less precise and includes almost any other activity that has not been accounted for in the national production, such as household chores. This last definition has implications when one considers differences in labor force participation by gender, insofar as the fraction of people who are engaged in household chores is still higher among women, especially in developing countries.

In real life, the decision to offer labor to a business is, of course, much more complex. Individuals are subject to many more limitations and needs, along with personal long-term goals and aspirations, that play an important role in their work-supply decision. This is the case with many other decisions or real-life situations that economic models intend to portray. The fact that economic models simplify reality helps explain why they do not provide exact predictions for real outcomes. This is especially relevant when we consider the role of models in the making of macroeconomic policy. However, one should keep in mind that models, although often inexact, tend to provide the closest mathematical approach to reality and facilitate decision-making.

Depending on the market wage, people spend part of their time working to earn income and allocate the rest of their time to leisure. The result is the labor supply, where the quantity offered depends on the real wage. Oddly, as has been discovered, higher wages do not always lead to a greater supply of labor. In fact, in some cases, higher hourly wages have null or even negative effects on the labor supply. This is because when real hourly wages increase, people who are already working and have a higher income can spend more during their free time, and so would not necessarily work more hours even if they were paid more per hour. In the following discussion, however, it will be assumed that the labor supply is a positive function of the real wage. In other words, we will assume that as real wages go up, so does the quantity of labor supplied.

The fact that economic models simplify reality helps explain why they do not provide exact predictions for real outcomes.

Now that we have determined labor demand and supply, the next step is to observe how they interact and how equilibrium is obtained in the *labor market*. Equilibrium is the point at which the demand for labor is met by the supply of labor: in other words, every job opening has been filled and the unemployment rate is 0 percent. True equilibrium is generally possible only in economic models. In the real world, there is often some level of unemployment, which we discuss in the next section. The simplest version of the labor market equilibrium is the classical approach, which assumes that real wages are flexible and adjust to keep the supply of and demand for labor in equilibrium. In this context, work is fully employed, since companies want to hire exactly the amount of work that people are offering, and the real wage is determined by the market.

Figure 3 shows how the labor market is balanced at the intersection of labor demand and supply. However, this relationship between output and employment could be broken temporarily. For example, in Chile, the year 2000 was quite contradictory in economic terms. While the Chilean GDP increased by 4.5 percent, 23,000 jobs were lost. This is paradoxical since historically, for every percentage point increase in Chile's GDP, employment grew by approximately 0.7 percent per year. This means that in the year 2000 more than 100,000 jobs should have been created.

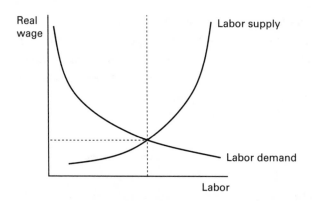

Figure 3 Relationship between output and employment.

From the above, it follows that, to have a more complete picture of the labor market, it is necessary to deepen the analysis beyond the level of employment. Not all types of work contribute equally to economic growth; hence a very relevant variable to better understand changes in the unemployment rate is the composition of employment. On some occasions, governments generate temporary public employment in response to periods of stagnation. Temporary public employment is on average less related to economic growth than is private employment. On the other hand, if a person obtains a job that does not allow her to fully use her productive skills, her contribution to production will be less. For example, when the economy slows down, some people are forced to reduce the number of hours they work per day, to accept employment in positions below their professional qualifications, or even to seek self-employment in the informal sector. In these situations the individual may be counted as employed but, strictly speaking, is underemployed.

The Unemployment Rate and Its Weaknesses

The *classical approach* discussed in the previous section considers that, given the adjustment of real wages, the economy will always be in full employment (at the level of *GDP of full employment*), although unemployment is an obvious phenomenon in the real world. How can we understand this apparent contradiction?

To begin with, it is important to note that part of unemployment corresponds to the normal rotation in the labor market, which lies behind the *natural rate of unemployment*. This unemployment rate is associated with the time it takes to bring together an employer who offers a job with an individual who seeks work according to his professional skills.

This time varies with the institutional characteristics of labor markets, such as social protection laws (e.g., a minimum wage law) and the bargaining power of labor unions, all of which raise hiring and dismissal costs, making the process of wage determination less flexible. The natural rate of unemployment prevails even in an economy where wages are completely flexible, but in general, the more flexible the process of wage determination, the lower this rate will be. Minimum wages, for example, although intended to guarantee a minimum standard of living for dependent workers, if higher than the market wage, can be a source of unemployment. This is particularly true in countries where the minimum wage is above the productivity of workers.

Markets where labor flows freely, that is, markets in which there are very few obstacles to hiring or firing workers, have lower unemployment rates than those in which strict regulations remain in place. The World Bank has developed an index that measures various aspects of the functioning of labor markets around the world. According to this index, countries such as the United States, Singapore, and Hong Kong have highly flexible labor markets, while countries such as Spain and France (among other European countries) have more rigid labor markets, notwithstanding the recent efforts of President Macron to increase flexibility.

Latin American countries also tend to show greater rigidities, as in the case of Argentina and Venezuela, where minimum wages have tended to be above the productivity of their workers. This has led to double-digit unemployment rates over the last few decades. Excessive labor regulations, in the end, lead workers to employment in the informal sector, where working conditions are more precarious. On the other hand, the evidence is mixed in the cases of Chile and Peru, which have a minimum wage closer to worker productivity than other countries in Latin America but still maintain high dismissal costs.

It is important to note that there are between-country differences in the measurement of the unemployment rate, according to criteria that classify workers as being inside or outside the labor market. In this respect, the following questions arise: Should a person who works a few hours a week be considered employed? What happens to those who, discouraged by not finding a job, simply stop looking for one and leave the workforce?

Such differences manifest themselves within a country as well. In Chile in 2002, for example, the National Employment Survey of the National Statistics Institute (INE) estimated that the unemployment rate in the Metropolitan Region was 8.6 percent, while the employment survey developed by the University of Chile indicated that the rate was around 13.3 percent. However, the official results of the General Population and Housing Census revealed that the effective unemployment rate reached 12.4 percent, much higher than the results of the census's usual unemployment survey and only slightly lower than the result obtained by the University of Chile. These differences are essentially explained by the difficulty in distinguishing between inactivity (being voluntarily out of work) and unemployment (being involuntarily unemployed), especially in the population younger than twenty-five years and in the population older than fifty-four years. This is a common problem in many countries.

Thus, comparing unemployment rates between countries is not as simple as it seems. For this reason, the International Labour Organization (ILO) attempts to reconcile these perspectives. Some regions have already done so. An example is the EU, which currently provides information on the *"harmonized" unemployment rate*, calculated with a similar measurement process for the EU's member nations.

In many countries, the unemployment rate is calculated from a monthly family survey conducted on a large scale (such surveys are typically referred to as *labor force surveys*). While household surveys are common in industrialized nations, alternative data collection methods are often used as a complement—and as a main source of unemployment information in many other countries. These alternative sources include a tally of people registered with the public employment service, information provided by unions on the status of their members, employers' lists, administrative counts of those receiving benefits, and the population census (which is generally carried out once every several years, typically once per decade).

In the United States, being unemployed is defined as not having paid employment and being actively looking for work in the most recent four weeks; waiting to start a job in the next four weeks; or being temporarily dismissed but waiting to return to the same job. However, the distinction between "being unemployed" and "actively seeking employment" is not always so clear in developing countries. For example, there may be a significant number of people employed for just a few hours a week, or engaged in activities of low productivity, such as street vendors. Hence it may be more useful to focus the analysis on *underemployment* rather than on unemployment. The reason for this is that people who are employed in activities that require fewer skills than they have, or fewer hours than they are willing to offer, are actually underemployed.

Another important distinction must be made between employment in the labor market and production outside the market (such as household chores). Female labor force participation is lower in many countries since household workers are not counted as part of the formal labor force, even though household work may be a more productive option than working in the market.

Another important phenomenon in developing countries that affects the unemployment rate is the existence of a significant number of "discouraged" workers, those who stop looking for work because they believe there are no vacancies available; and of workers in the informal (unregulated) sector and in the black market, who do their best to ensure that their activities are kept secret.

Differences in how data on unemployment in developed countries are interpreted also arise. For example, Japan, Sweden, the Netherlands, and Switzerland have reported relatively low rates of unemployment for many years, though often for reasons that are far from evident in the data.

For example, many Japanese women operate with short-term employment contracts and leave the labor force when their jobs disappear during recessions, and so are not counted as unemployed. In Sweden, the government has traditionally used aggressive employment and job training programs to absorb those who do not find work in the private sector. Whether these are "real jobs" or just a way to reduce the unemployment figures in the official statistics is a matter of opinion.

In addition, programs for the disabled increased in Holland, along with deteriorating working conditions, and many of those dismissed were reclassified as disabled rather than unemployed. In Switzerland, foreign workers were invited to leave the country after an economic recession in the mid-1970s. In each of the above cases, the low unemployment rates are not what they seem at first glance.

Other technical differences in the definition of unemployment lead to variations in rates in different countries. Economies differ, for example, in the age limit at which someone is counted as unemployed. The types of activity that are understood as "actively seeking" also vary, as well as the metric of people who have been laid off for a while. There are also differences in how to account for activities such as working in the military, on a family farm, or in domestic service, as well as how to account for students, because when they look for employment certain countries register them as unemployed and others do not.

"Standardized" unemployment rates, such as those recorded by the Organisation for Economic Co-operation and Development (OECD), incorporate many such comparability problems and provide a useful and reliable indicator of differences between countries. However, while such measurements may be standardized, it is still useful to think that there may be an underlying measurement problem even after the harmonization.

It should be noted that when the labor force undergoes major changes, the unemployment rate does not fully reveal the labor market situation. In other words, the unemployment rate can behave in a way that does not accurately or timely reflect the creation or disappearance of jobs. For example, when the unemployment rate is high for several consecutive periods it is possible that two opposing effects appear. One is linked to the fact that when the head of the household loses his or her job, other family members who do not participate in any paid work activity, such as housewives, retirees, or students, try to work to compensate for the drop in family income. This effect, called the *additional worker effect*, would continue to raise the unemployment rate. This is because not only are people losing their jobs (in this case, the head of the household), but others who were outside the labor force (other family members) suddenly start searching for work, increasing the number of overall unemployed. On the other hand, if someone has lost a job and the search for a new one has not been successful, that person may choose to use the time of waiting for domestic and training activities, which means a decrease in the workforce. This effect, known as the *discouraged worker effect*, decreases the unemployment rate.

Which of the two effects predominates? It varies from one period to another and from one country to another. For example, there is evidence of the additional worker effect in Argentina during the 1990s, whereas in Chile in 2000 the discouraged worker effect seemed more pronounced.

On the other hand, as discussed in the previous section, the rise in unemployment is linked to the economic cycle, and specifically to recessions. Once recovery begins, it is possible to expect a decrease in the unemployment rate. However, a rise in the unemployment rate may produce lasting effects on the "natural" (or full) employment rate, a phenomenon that economists call *hysteresis*. (More generally, hysteresis denotes the continuation of effects after the causes of those effects have been removed.) In real life hysteresis arises because, in certain circumstances, unemployed individuals gradually lose the skills obtained in a previous job or move away from previous contact and information networks of the labor market, and for these reasons continue to remain unemployed.

Not all increases in unemployment are necessarily linked to recessive periods. What reasons, then, could explain such rises? The explanations are varied and include, among others:

• An increase in the minimum wage, which strongly affects those with lower qualifications, especially younger people.

• Structural changes, such as the process of globalization, which has pushed a need for cost reduction to maintain or improve competitiveness and has led companies to reduce personnel and merge; or the appearance of technological progress that leaves some companies obsolete, leading to their closure and their workers unemployed. Nonetheless, in a dynamic economy, the creation of new jobs will overcome the destruction of jobs.

• Uncertainty about the course of events, caused by both internal sources (e.g., a policy reform that makes hiring or firing workers more difficult) and external sources (e.g., a war or possible global recession), hinders the hiring of new employees. For example, in the United States in 2007, before the financial crisis unfolded, the unemployment rate stood at 4.7 percent. In August 2008, before markets collapsed and panic spread, the rate was already at 6.2 percent. In other economies of the world, a similar process of increased unemployment occurred during 2008 and 2009. Of course, when this uncertainty materialized in an adverse scenario, the unemployment rate increased much more, but the fact remains that uncertainty tends to paralyze new activities, and therefore inhibits job creation. One of the main lessons to be drawn from international evidence is that when labor markets are more flexible, unemployment becomes less persistent. In the United States, perhaps the most flexible labor market in the world, people who lose a job hope to find a new one in just a few months; in contrast, in some European countries characterized by high labor rigidity, someone who loses his or her job must prepare to be unemployed for a period of two or three years.

Consider the case of Spain, which in the last thirty-six years had only four recessions (1981, 1993, 2009, and 2011–2013), defined as a decline in GDP for two consecutive quarters. However, Spain's unemployment rate has for a long time been the highest among EU countries. This is mainly due to the rigidity of the Spanish labor market, exemplified by the generous unemployment insurance, which discourages the search for a new job, and the high power of labor union groups after the political transition post-Franco.

During the recession of 2009, Spain experienced several consecutive periods of negative economic growth and unemployment rates above 20 percent. In this case, the rigidity of the labor market was combined with the restrictions imposed by a single currency. However, since 2013 there has been a downward trend in the unemployment rate, in line with the implementation of a labor reform in 2012, which reduced severance pay, encouraged hiring for indefinite terms, and provided facilities to companies to modify shift systems and the remuneration of their employees, among other modifications.

WHY AND HOW DO
COUNTRIES GROW?

The process of economic growth is defined as the sustained increase in the output of a country or region. It is usually measured as the increase in real gross domestic product (GDP) over a period of time, which could be a few years or even decades.

In 1980, China's average annual per capita income was close to US $310, while a Bolivian national had an average annual income of US $2,090 and someone from Venezuela had an income of US $7,838 (all figures expressed in purchasing power parity, or PPP, dollars, as explained in chapter 1). That is, the average income of a Chinese citizen was one-seventh that of a Bolivian and one-twenty-fifth that of a Venezuelan.

By 2017, China's per capita income was about twenty-one times the 1980 figure, while Bolivia's average income had grown slowly and Venezuela's income had decreased over the same period. Thus today an average Chinese citizen has more than twice the income of a Bolivian, and also more than the average income of a Venezuelan. What is surprising is that such dramatic changes in the relative living standards of these countries occurred within a relatively short period—only three decades.

Cases of rapid *economic growth* for some countries and economic stagnation or decline for others are far from isolated. While Chile and Ecuador had similar incomes in 1980, today an average Chilean lives with more than twice the income of the average Ecuadorean. Similarly, in 1980 South Korea had a per capita income one quarter that of Spain, whereas today a Korean has a slightly higher income than a Spaniard. What are the causes of such differences? Why do some countries grow so much more than others? What should a country do to grow more?

Growth rates and real GDP levels differ substantially from one economy to another, resulting in huge differences in per capita income between countries—the per capita income in Luxembourg is more than three hundred times that of Burundi. And even though the difference is much lower when measured in PPP terms, Luxembourg's average income is still more than one hundred times Burundi's.

Note that slight differences in annual growth rates have a strong impact on the level of per capita income over a long period. With per capita growth of 1 percent a year, it takes about seventy years to double the average income per person; however, if growth is 3 percent per annum, a country will have to wait only twenty-three years to double its per capita income; and if the rate reaches 7 percent annually, per capita income doubles in just a decade.

In what follows, we highlight the changes experienced by an economy over several decades (in the long term), and therefore the short-term fluctuations known as business cycles will not be considered. This does not mean that business cycles do not affect economic growth. In this respect, recent studies indicate that in the long run, countries with the most volatile economies, or the highest frequency of economic fluctuations, experience less economic growth than countries that are more stable.

Modern Economic Growth

To understand the changes in the material wealth of the world, we must begin by examining development over the centuries. Table 3 shows the evolution of world population and per capita output in the last two thousand years. Note that the real leap forward occurred in the last phase, when the per capita output growth rate increased to almost 1.3 percent per year and the population grew at more than double its growth rate in the previous stage. This jump

Table 3 Population and per capita GDP growth in the last twenty centuries (annual average)

Economic phase	Period	Rate of population increase	GDP per capita (%)
Agricultural economy	0–1500	0.04	0.01
Advanced agricultural economy	1500–1700	0.16	0.04
Merchant capitalism	1700–1820	0.46	0.07
Capitalism	1820–2017	1.06	1.26

Source: For years 0–2010, Maddison, *Phases of Capitalist Development*; for years 2010–2016, International Monetary Fund, *World Economic Outlook 2018*.

coincides with the Industrial Revolution, when modern economic growth began.

As an economy enters the last stage of growth, it undergoes important changes in its economic structure. As a result, we observe some common patterns in different countries and regions. The characteristics of this common process are the following:

• In growing economies, the relative size of the agricultural sector in the economy tends to decline. Thus, whereas in 1810, 70 percent of the US labor force was engaged in agriculture, that figure now stands at barely 1 percent.

• In the early stages of accelerated growth, the industrial sector increases rapidly, peaks, and then its share in the economy tends to decline. At the same time, the services sector grows steadily and increases its participation in the economy as industry and agriculture reduce theirs.

• Another pattern in development is *urbanization*, defined as population concentration in relatively large and dense settlements. In Chile, more than 70 percent of the population lived in rural areas in 1865. By 1907, the urban population constituted 43 percent of the total, and by 2015, 87 percent of the population lived in urban areas. In the entire world in 1880 the urban population was around 8 percent. Worldwide, urbanization surpassed the 50 percent mark for the first time in history at some point around 1990. The growth of cities is a consequence of the decline of agriculture and the growth of industry and the services sector.

• Another characteristic of economic growth is an increase in the *division of labor* and *specialization*. This stems from the increasing ability of individuals to specialize in a relatively narrow range of economic activities, thereby acquiring specific skills. However, in most poor economies there tends to be little specialization: most of the workers carry out a wide range of activities, from growing vegetables to preparing food, building houses, raising animals, making and mending clothing, and many other things. Although such self-sufficiency allows them to survive, though at a very low level of material welfare, greater specialization becomes crucial for progress. In other words, workers gradually and conveniently switch their focus to fewer tasks, which in turn becomes possible thanks to trade. Even in the most primitive trade systems, people come together to offer something in exchange for something else they need, so they do not have to produce all the goods they consume. The continuous deepening and perfecting of specialization and trade have joined to deliver our current capitalist system.

• *Technological progress*, which results in the creation of new products, as well as the ability to produce at lower cost, is one of the most important drivers of economic growth. While there are many sources of technological progress, research and development (R&D) efforts are undoubtedly the most important. However, societies differ markedly from one another in terms of resources devoted to R&D. Rich countries usually allocate between 2 percent and 5 percent of GDP to R&D, distributing it among industrial laboratories, universities, and state research institutions. In contrast, poor nations generally allocate resources well below 1 percent of their GDP to such efforts. And since the per capita GDP of a poor country often amounts to one-tenth (or less) that of a rich country, the per capita expenditure gap in R&D often shows a difference of greater than twenty or thirty times.

Malthus and the Asian Tigers

At the end of the eighteenth century, following years in which the economy grew very slowly, important analysts doubted that economic growth would ever be enough to support the rapidly increasing population. Thomas Malthus, a famous British thinker, viewed the population increase occurring in Britain with great pessimism. In addition, he was convinced that per capita GDP would fall under the weight of a demographic explosion. According to his point of view, if the population exceeded the economic capacity, then the number of inhabitants would be adjusted, if not by wars, by disasters such as famines or epidemics. In his own words:

> The power of population is so superior to the power
> in the earth to produce subsistence for man that
> premature death must in some shape or other visit
> the human race. The vices of mankind are active
> and able ministers of depopulation. They are
> the precursors in the great army of destruction,
> and often finish the dreadful work themselves. But
> should they fail in this war of extermination, sickly
> seasons, epidemics, pestilence and plague advance
> in terrific array, and sweep off their thousands and

tens of thousands. Should success still be incomplete, gigantic inevitable famine stalks in the rear, and with one mighty blow levels the population with the food of the world. (Malthus, "First Essay on Population 1798")

Fortunately, Malthus committed one of the most important prediction errors in world economic history. Although some regions have advanced much more than others, the global economy has generally experienced sustained and unprecedented economic growth over the last two centuries. One notable case is that of the so-called Asian tigers—South Korea, Hong Kong, Taiwan, and Singapore. These countries were essentially poor economies dependent on foreign aid in the early 1960s; however, between 1960 and 2000, their GDP per capita increased, on average, at a rate of 6 percent per year. These figures are even more impressive compared to the 1.6 percent per annum observed in Latin America and the 2.7 percent per annum experienced by industrialized nations that are members of the Organisation for Economic Co-operation and Development (OECD) for that same period. In South Korea, for example, per capita GDP grew at an average annual rate of 5.9 percent during those four decades. In other words, in just over a generation the average Korean became ten times richer!

Although the subject has been much discussed, there is some consensus on the factors that promoted this "miracle" in Asian nations. A well-known World Bank study from 1993, *The East Asian Miracle*, found that domestic private investment and the rapid growth of human capital (the investment in education and training programs, which increases the productive capacity of the labor force), sustained by high saving rates, served as the growth engine. To this one must add the presence of stable macroeconomic policies, trade liberalization, and a well-qualified labor force.

The world's population grew rapidly in the last hundred years, from about 1.6 billion people in 1900 to almost 8.3 billion in 2016. According to a United Nations projection, there will be 9.1 billion people by 2050. As a result, there will be increasing pressure on terrestrial ecology and essential natural resources such as drinking water and biological diversity in the tropics. This, however, is not enough to support Malthus's claim.

Sources of Growth

In the previous chapter, we indicated that the production function is the relationship between output, production inputs, and technology. In this relationship, output growth is often linked to the degree of technological innovation and to the growth of capital and labor in the economy.

Labor and capital shares are measured in the national accounts. In most Latin American countries, the share of income from labor (i.e., the sum of a country's citizens' work income) as a percentage of total GDP is low compared to that of developed countries mainly because labor is relatively abundant and wages are low. Additionally, the share or labor income as a percentage of total GDP may also be low owing to the existence of self-employment and small businesses, which, if not correctly accounted for, hides from the statistician what percentage of income corresponds to wages and how much corresponds to the profits from personal activities.

Let us clarify this point with an example. Assume that the share of labor production of GDP is 40 percent, while the share of capital is 60 percent. Now, suppose that the labor force increases by 1.8 percent annually, technology grows by 1.6 percent, and the capital stock grows by 4.2 percent. In this case, we would predict an annual increase in GDP of 4.8 percent (1.6% + (0.4 × 1.8%) + (0.6 × 4.2%)).

An interesting case is that of Chile, where the labor share in GDP is estimated at around 52 percent. Between 1986 and 2015, employment increased by 2.5 percent annually, the capital stock grew at an average rate of 4.9 percent, and *total factor productivity* (TFP) grew at around 1.3 percent. TFP is the component of economic growth that is not explained by an increase in the productive factors (capital and labor); thus TFP is interpreted as the fraction of economic growth attributable to technological progress. We would formulate annual GDP growth as 1.3% + (0.52 × 2.5%) + (0.48 × 4.9%) = 5.0 percent per year. However, this average of two decades hides very diverse behaviors: between 1986 and 1996 GDP grew at an annual average of 7.3 percent and productivity grew at 3.4 percent; in the following decade (1997–2007), GDP increased at 4.2 percent and productivity at 0.77 percent; while in the last years (2008–2015), GDP grew by 3.4 percent and productivity decreased by 0.36 percent (all figures are annual averages). The previous analysis reveals that in recent years, not only did TFP not contribute, on average, to economic growth, it decreased it. This observation highlights the importance of technological progress as a fundamental driver of growth in a country. Technological progress is understood as improvement in the tools needed for the production process, from computational software and programs to specific abilities and knowledge.

Robert Solow, winner of the Nobel Prize in Economics for his contributions to growth theory and its measurement, first used his analysis to measure the sources of US growth between 1909 and 1949. His results were surprising: he estimated that technological progress was responsible for 88 percent of economic growth.

On the other hand, a study of the sources of economic growth in the seven largest Latin American economies since the 1940s concluded that capital accumulation accounted for a much larger fraction of per capita GDP growth than did technological progress.

There is an interesting debate as to the sources of accelerated growth experienced by some developing countries, particularly the Asian tigers discussed earlier in this chapter. From the early 1960s to 2010, the per capita output of many Asian countries grew at rates above 5 percent per year, the highest in history for such a prolonged period.

One of the most controversial issues is whether Asia grew as a result of greater accumulation of productive factors or whether the growth was due to technological modernization. The evidence indicates that both aspects played important roles, although the accumulation of productive factors (labor and capital) has predominated in some countries.

Recent studies of economic growth suggest that capital, including human capital (i.e., the value brought by well-educated, well-trained workers), may play a more important role than is suggested by current economic models. The basic notion of these new studies is that capital investment, whether in machinery or in people, improves not only the productive capacity of the company or the worker but also the productive capacity of other companies and other related workers. In economic jargon, this benefit for others is known as a *positive externality*. This could happen if, for example, there are spillovers of knowledge between companies and workers who are using the new technologies. In this sense, if a company acquires new knowledge, other nearby companies could also benefit from it. Such knowledge spillovers help explain why high-tech companies tend to cluster in specific areas, such as Silicon Valley near San Francisco and Route 128 around Boston in the United States.

Factors behind Economic Growth

Savings and investment decisions, as well as the efficiency of such investments, depend to a large extent on *economic policies*, institutions, and even the physical geography of a country or region.

There is now enough evidence to identify the key empirical factors that best explain the growth of different countries over the past forty years.

• Economic policies are fundamental to growth. For example, countries that maintain open markets, both for domestic and for international trade, are generally more successful than more closed economies, where the government actively participates in production and places restrictions on markets. This seems to be the case in Southeast Asian economies, where the size of the countries' trade (the sum of exports and imports) greatly exceeds the value of their GDP. This result is a useful measure of the value of market openness, where trading for more than the value of the GDP indicates that the welfare of a country's citizens exceeds that which they would have if the GDP were limited to only national production, and more specifically, it is significantly benefited from international production. For example, in 2015, Malaysia's trade was around 1.3 times GDP, in Singapore it was 3.3 times GDP, and in Hong Kong it was no less than 4 times the value of GDP. This degree of openness is far from the Latin American average, where trade accounts for only about 40 percent of GDP (0.4 the value of GDP).

• *Political and economic institutions* are also decisive factors for growth. For example, countries with a written constitution and where an independent judicial system enforces contracts fairly and within the law tend to show better growth indicators than countries where the government operates outside the law or is corrupt. On the other hand, countries with low bureaucratic costs present better performance than their counterparts, which hinder entrepreneurship by imposing excessive amounts of paperwork and regulations, which drives away investors. Another important element is economic stability, which is key to eliminating unnecessary uncertainty, which may inhibit profitable projects and, therefore, economic growth. Some key economic institutions needed to achieve economic stability are an independent central bank and, in some cases, specific institutional fiscal rules that help provide greater stability to a country.

• Certain *structural characteristics* also affect growth. Geographic features such as country location, climate, and access to ports affect the costs inherent in trade, labor productivity, and the returns on agriculture, among other factors. For example, several tropical countries have lower productivity as a result of the existence of infectious diseases such as malaria, which is concentrated in warm areas and causes permanent disruptions in people's lives, impairing growth. Other geographic characteristics such as the lack of access to ports generate greater costs in international trade through hindering countries' ability to connect with the rest of the world, and possibly obstruct the attainment of superior rates of growth.

The Prevalence of Policies and Institutions over Culture

The evidence suggests that the growth of an economy depends more on the institutions and policies that are implemented than on the cultural characteristics of the population.

The case of North and South Korea is a good example of this thesis. In 1945, at the end of World War II, the Korean Peninsula was artificially divided in two, north and south. The former was initially occupied by the Soviet Union and the latter was dominated by the United States. Before that, the peninsula had been a unified territory for centuries; hence, inhabitants on both sides shared the same cultural codes, customs, traditions, and even festivities. However, while South Korea began to implement pro-market institutions that promoted competition and allowed the free flow of goods, capital, and people, North Korea instead established a centralized system that imposed severe restrictions on the economy.

The diverging paths of development that the two parts of the peninsula followed speaks for itself. In 1990, forty-five years after the division, the per capita GDP of South Korea was already six times that of North Korea. By 2016, the per capita GDP of South Korea was more than twenty times that of North Korea. East and West Germany represented a similar case right up to the fall of the Berlin Wall in 1991. In 1990 the pro-market Federal Republic of Germany, or West Germany, had a per capita GDP almost four times that of the German Democratic Republic (East Germany). These examples clearly illustrate that the growth of an economy depends more on its institutions than on cultural factors.

These examples clearly illustrate that the growth of an economy depends more on its institutions than on cultural factors.

Studies on the matter during the last decade have provided this theory with robust empirical evidence. The distinguished MIT economist Daron Acemoglu and his British colleague, James Robinson, are outstanding contributors to this topic. They used historical data and sophisticated empirical methods to conclude that the main determinant of differences in prosperity across countries is differences in institutions. According to their findings, achieving greater economic growth and prosperity requires reforming institutions, something that depends heavily on political processes.

Following the thesis supported by Acemoglu and Robinson, China gives reason for debate. Between 1980 and 2010, the Chinese economy grew at an impressive average rate of 10 percent, and at a no less impressive rate of 7.5 percent between 2011 and 2017. On the other hand, one must consider the significant influence the Chinese government still maintains over some areas of production. When this control is considered along with the facts that capital does not flow freely and that political institutions are far from transparent, one might have reason to doubt that institutions are really the greatest determinant of countries' development. However, although China does not have "optimal" economic or political institutions, the country has enacted substantial reforms in recent decades in the direction of a more open and decentralized economy. These reforms were critical for greater productivity growth, a key driver of China's economic performance. Thus the case of China reaffirms the importance of institutions to achieving economic prosperity.

Natural Resources and Economic Growth

Whether natural resources are a factor that contributes to economic growth has long been debated in economics. Intuitively, a country endowed with large reserves of natural resources should be able to obtain large revenues by exploiting them, thus becoming richer than other countries. However, several studies have shown that economies with abundant natural resources tend to grow less than resource-scarce economies, a phenomenon known as the *resource curse*. Researchers who have explored this phenomenon include Sachs and Warner; Boschini, Pettersson, and Roine; and Van der Ploeg.

Several theories attempt to explain why resource revenues may have an adverse effect on economic growth. Some authors have pointed out that the intrinsic volatility associated with the price of natural resources increases overall volatility in the country, thus affecting investment decisions. Natural resource revenues may also generate incentives for rent-seeking, which occurs when entrepreneurs find it more profitable to lobby in order to obtain a portion of the resource rents instead of engaging in productive activities. Other studies have highlighted the political effects of an abundance of natural resources, since large resource revenues may lead to corruption or may be used to gain political support instead of improving local living standards.

There is probably no unique explanation for the resource curse; however, most authors agree that a resource-abundant country is not condemned to poor economic performance. There are many resource-abundant countries with low economic development, such as Sierra Leone, Bolivia, and the Democratic Republic of Congo, though other resource-abundant countries have successfully promoted economic growth, such as Norway, Australia, and Botswana. Countries that have exploited their abundant natural resource endowments and simultaneously accomplished economic development were most likely able to do so because of the quality of their economic and political institutions.

Once again, institutions are a key determinant of differences in prosperity across countries. Solid macroeconomic institutions will help reduce the volatility associated with the international price of natural resources, well-stablished property rights will avoid rent-seeking incentives, and government accountability and transparency will reduce corruption.

MONEY, INFLATION, AND THE EXCHANGE RATE

Four hundred years ago, Spain's Francisco de Quevedo wrote, "Over kings and priests and scholars, rules the mighty Lord of Money," which still seems to be true today. Money gives purchasing power over resources, and its rate of expansion (the rate at which it grows) is closely related to inflation.

In this chapter, we analyze how monetary authorities regulate the circulation of money and the relationship between money and economic activity. Additionally, two closely related issues are studied: price determination and the role of the *exchange rate*, after which we can understand what sometimes motivates governments to abandon the use of one currency in favor of another—the French franc for the euro, or the Ecuadoran sucre for the dollar. The study of these topics will also help us understand the reasons for the current discussion of the role of the dollar as the world's reserve currency and the competition it faces from the euro, the yuan, the yen, the pound, and other currencies.

How the exchange rate should be managed is a matter that is permanently discussed by economic authorities across the world. At the turn of the twenty-first century, however, the discussion became ever more heated as a result of the accelerated globalization process, substantial growth volume, and the deepening of financial relations.

Money

Money serves as a *means of exchange* for goods and services, thereby eliminating the need for barter, and as an accounting unit. Money also serves as a *unit of account* because all goods can be expressed in monetary terms; thus only a single price for each good is required for transactions to occur.

Therefore, prices are the rate at which money is exchanged for goods. Money also serves in certain circumstances as means to *store value*: the bills and coins that someone carries in her pocket today will probably have the same value a week later, in terms of their ability to acquire goods. As a store of value, money has some advantages over other assets, such as being the most liquid of all; also, its nominal value in the future is not subject to uncertainty (as is often the case with different financial instruments such as futures and derivatives). However, as we shall see below, inflation deteriorates the value of money as a store of wealth.

Money is crucial for the development of commercial and financial transactions in any modern economy. Without money, operations would have to be done through barter. Although it may sound like something of the past, barter is still used in some situations. For example, in early 2002 Argentina was in a deep crisis and lacked means of payment as a result of the "*corralito*," a measure that prevented checking account and deposit holders from withdrawing funds from banks. Under these circumstances, in places like small public markets, barter was used to carry out smaller economic transactions. Another example is Zimbabwe, which until 2009 suffered from huge price instability, facing both a terrible hyperinflation and repeated deflations (or negative inflation), and so, since people did not want to keep local currency, many turned to barter for everyday transactions. The case of Venezuela is more recent: after experiencing an inflation rate above 1,000,000 percent by the end of 2018, combined with a shortage of products in the formal market, people began using barter to acquire basic consumption goods.

However, barter is extremely inefficient, because it requires a mutual coincidence of needs. For example, a sick painter would need a doctor willing to treat him in exchange for one of his paintings. In addition, the price of each good would need to be fixed in terms of all others; people would have to calculate and agree on how many hens are equivalent to a chair, how many to a lecture on economics, and so on.

The History of Money and Gresham's Law

From the dawn of human history, societies have recognized the many inconveniences of barter, so they have turned to money. Although it is not clear when some form of money was first used, we know that metallic money began to be used around 5000–6000 BCE.

While metals offer many advantages over forms of money other than bills, all sorts of commodities have been used as money throughout history: colored seashells in India, cigarettes in the prison camps of World War II, and even whale's teeth in Fiji.

Gresham's law helps explain societal shifts toward current forms of money. It is named after Sir Thomas Gresham, founder of the Royal London Stock Exchange, who famously stated that "bad money drives out good." By this he was referring to a money system based on nonstandard objects, where, for example, if gold and chicken are the two forms of money in circulation, the more valuable of the two will disappear from circulation. This law constitutes an interesting facet of the historical use of money.

For example, at one time in Tanzania, livestock served as money, and soon people realized that only the weakest and sickest animals were being used in transactions. The reason was very simple: the value of goods and services was expressed in number of heads of cattle, without distinguishing between good and bad ones. Since livestock has an intrinsic value for its meat, milk, leather, and transportation services, it was more convenient to pay with the faulty cattle and keep the healthy ones. This explains why societies increasingly turned to standardizing and certifying forms of money based on precious metals.

Coinage emerged in Greece in the seventh century BCE and proved to be a useful way to relieve this problem, so it quickly became popular. Coins substantially reduced the need to weigh and certify the metals, thereby facilitating transactions. For about four hundred years, until the third century BCE, the Athenian drachma kept its silver content virtually unchanged and was by far the predominant currency of the Old World.

In the days of their empire, the Romans introduced a bimetallic system made up of the silver denarius and the golden aureus. During the first century CE, at the time of the notorious emperor Nero, the amount of precious metal contained in such coins began to decrease as both gold and silver were increasingly combined with alloys.

Not surprisingly, the prices of goods expressed in these units rose at unprecedented rates. After this inflationary process, there were growing fiscal deficits that the Roman government was unable to eliminate through spending controls or tax increases.

Although other metals were also used, gold and silver remained the most common metals used as money for a long time. In the battle between silver and gold, silver prevailed during the second half of the sixteenth century: the recently discovered New World proved to hold greater riches in silver than in gold, especially after the exploitation of silver mines in Potosi, Bolivia, and Zacatecas, Mexico.

Paper money gained momentum in the late eighteenth century. It first took the form of *backed money* as paper certificates that promised to pay a specific amount of gold or silver. These obligations were issued by private agents (companies and banks), but with time, the government's role became increasingly important in their usage. At the same time, another form of paper money appeared, so-called *fiduciary money*, the value of which depended on people's agreement and trust that it stored value despite not representing any amount of gold, silver, or other merchandise. Its value arose simply from its acceptance by other agents as a means of payment.

In the second half of the nineteenth century, the world witnessed a massive transition to the *gold standard*.

In this system, coins and notes were converted into gold according to an established parity metric. By the end of the century, the use of silver for monetary contracts was sharply reduced. Of all the great nations, only China continued to have a bimetallic system based on gold and silver.

With the outbreak of World War I, most countries suspended the convertibility of their gold coins, and the gold standard collapsed. Attempts to reinstall the system after the war were unsuccessful; moreover, at a time when only fiduciary money was in circulation, the Great Depression and World War II made the collapse of the gold standard definite. Toward the end of World War II, in 1944, monetary arrangements were again organized. The Bretton Woods Agreement led to widespread acceptance of a US dollar–based monetary pattern whereby the major currencies were backed by the dollar at a specific but adjustable rate, while the dollar was convertible into gold at the price of $35 an ounce. The Bretton Woods Agreement collapsed in 1971, when US president Richard Nixon suspended the dollar's convertibility to gold. Since then the world has lived with a mixed system of different national fiduciary currencies, with flexible exchange rates between major currencies, and where some nations promise to convert their currencies into dollars or other currencies at a fixed parity. In January 1999 a group of eleven European countries adopted the euro as a single common currency, to be

traded freely against the dollar, the yen, and other currencies. Today nineteen countries have adopted the euro. As
we will see later in this chapter, adopting a single currency
is a way of fixing the exchange rate.

The Money Market and the Inflation Rate

Money, like most goods and services, is traded in a market where supply and demand determine the amount of
money that people and companies use. In this case, the
money market does not necessarily need a physical place.

How is the *demand for money* determined? Economic
agents need a certain amount of money to carry out their
transactions; at the same time, keeping cash means losing the interest that money would earn if, for example, it
were deposited in a savings account. These two factors determine how much money people and companies want to
hold. Consequently, it is expected that there will be a relationship between the growth of money (i.e., the expansion
of the amount of money in circulation, or monetary base)
and the expansion of economic activity.

The *money supply* is determined by the emission of
coins and banknotes for circulation. In general, countries
have a central bank, a single official institution with legal
authority to issue money. This institution receives different names in different countries: the Federal Reserve in

the United States (the Fed), the European Central Bank, the Bank of Japan, the Central Bank of the Argentine Republic, the Central Bank of Chile, or the Bank of Mexico, to name a few.

Until a few decades ago, in most countries the issuance of money was determined mainly by the supply of goods such as gold or silver. When paper money was used, it was usually backed by precious metals at a fixed rate.

Today, however, the money of a country is backed fundamentally by the confidence of economic agents in the "quality" of the issuer (the central bank). This confidence is only partially based on the reserves held by the central bank in gold and is mainly backed by other financial products, such as treasury bonds.

Money market equilibrium occurs when the supply of and the demand for money are matched. If such a balance is disturbed, for example if the central bank issues more money than economic agents wish to keep, the result is an excess supply of money. In a *closed economy* (one that does not carry out commercial or financial transactions with the rest of the world) or in an open economy with a free exchange rate, the money market equilibrium is restored by an increase in prices—in other words, inflation. Thus, changes in the money supply that are not demanded translate into higher prices. In most cases, high inflation occurs because the government finances its excess spending by printing more money.

Today the money of a country is backed fundamentally by the confidence of economic agents in the "quality" of the issuer (the central bank).

This sort of situation highlights the importance of an autonomous central bank, so that the government is not permitted to manipulate the money supply to fit its financial needs. When a central bank is not autonomous, persistent fiscal deficits may lead to a constant growth of the money supply and high inflation rates, as will be discussed with further details in the next chapters. Managing the money supply is an important part of monetary policy.

Monetary Policy

Monetary policy is the specific macroeconomic policy that the central bank (the monetary authority) uses to manage the money supply to maintain economic stability. An autonomous central bank is one that operates monetary policy without the intervention of the local government—or any other economic agent.

The central bank's objective is to ensure the stability of the currency, which requires keeping inflation low and stable over time. The central bank must also promote the stability and efficiency of the financial system, ensuring the normal functioning of national and international payments. In achieving these objectives, the central bank contributes to laying the foundations for sustained economic growth by creating a predictable environment for decision-making.

To do this, most central banks mainly manage the interest rate by moving it upward or downward. When the objective is to increase the amount of money in circulation (or *monetary base*), it is called an expansionary monetary policy, and implies lowering the interest rate so that it becomes cheaper to borrow money and keeping money in a savings account is less attractive. A restrictive monetary policy aims to reduce the amount of money in circulation and implies raising the interest rate, making it more expensive to borrow money and increasing the incentives for saving.

Another means by which the central bank affects the amount of money in circulation (the monetary base) is through imposing liquidity requirements on private banks. These liquidity requirements are implemented mainly through the imposition of a *reserve requirement*, a minimum amount of reserves in cash that private banks must keep in their vaults. This restrains the amount of money private banks can lend to the public. A higher reserve requirement implies that banks can lend less money to the public because for every certain amount of money that is deposited in the bank, a higher fraction of it must be kept as a reserve and not lent to customers.

However, the monetary *base* is different from the money *supply*. Moreover, the monetary base, once determined by the central bank, is later "multiplied" by the actions of commercial banks and the public, which we call the *money multiplier* or multiplier effect. The money multiplier is greater when the same amount of money circulates more times in the economy and the smaller the reserve requirement. For example, let's say the reserve requirement is 20 percent, and a bank receives a deposit for $100. Then $20 must be kept in reserve and the remaining $80 may be lent to other bank customers. The $80 may be then deposited by this third party. The bank into which the $80 has been deposited must keep $16 as a reserve and may lend out the remaining $64. The cycle repeats: the $64 may be deposited by another person into this (or another bank), out of which the bank must reserve $12.80 and may lend $51.20. To this point in the example we have accumulated a total of $244 in deposits, created from an initial deposit of $100. This is the multiplier effect: banks successively receive deposits, reserve what is required, and lend out to other customers.

However, in this example of the money multiplier, we have not yet considered the potential productive uses to which money could be put by bank customers or the interest paid (charged) to depositors (creditors). For example, a deposit in a commercial bank (from a depositor) can be turned into part of a loan to a third party to buy a car and become a taxi driver (creditor). The taxi driver will be charged interest as part of his or her debt to the bank, which he or she will gradually repay until the debt is completely paid off, at which point the taxi business begins to deliver profits. These profits may be reinvested in the taxi business, perhaps to buy another taxi or even to hire a driver for the car, leaving the owner free to engage in other productive activities. On the other hand, deposits made in commercial banks receive a prize (or interest); hence, by the time the depositor returns for his or her money, he or she will receive whatever was initially deposited plus the interest promised in exchange for the deposit. Simultaneously other people may make deposits in this bank, which enables the bank to manage the timing of debt repayment and deposit withdrawals, and the interest rates that will be offered to other parties. The more times the money circulates in the economy, the greater the money multiplier. In this case, a single deposit spurred profits for at least two more people beyond the initial depositor.

While the main instrument used by monetary policy is the short-term interest rate, following the financial crisis of 2008, several of the world's major central banks adopted alternative instruments, which are referred to as unconventional monetary policy tools.

Unconventional Monetary Policy

As we mentioned earlier, a traditional mechanism of monetary policy is to reduce interest rates to stimulate economic activity by making it less expensive to borrow money and leaving money in a savings account a less attractive option. However, when there is no further room for a reduction in rates, as in the United States following the Great Recession in 2008, when interest rates fell to a range of 0 to 0.25 percent, the US Federal Reserve pursued a program called *quantitative easing* (QE), which entailed the purchase of long-term financial assets such as government bonds and mortgage-backed securities to expand the money supply and thus lessen the severity of the recession.

The QE program had three stages, during the years 2008 (QE1), 2010 (QE2), and 2012 (QE3), and then began its retreat in 2014. Led by Fed chairman Ben Bernanke, QE was initially viewed with skepticism in some academic circles as an explosive increase in the monetary base could possibly accelerate inflation, although these concerns never materialized. The money injected was quickly absorbed by economic agents, who grew more risk-averse during the crisis, and thus increased their demand for cash.

As the effects of the crisis spread to the rest of the world, unconventional monetary policies such as those applied by the Fed were introduced by the central banks of other affected economies. Thus in 2011 the European Central Bank (ECB) began providing liquidity to commercial banks through a long-term refinancing program known as LTRO. This program consisted of a sort of auction of funds, where banks were refinancing themselves at lower interest rates, on the order of 1 percent, and had a second version in 2012, allocating more than €3,000 billion to about eight hundred commercial banks.

Exchange Rate Systems

In an open economy, an additional variable needs to be considered: the exchange rate. The exchange rate measures the market value of the national currency in relation to a foreign currency. This variable has been a permanent topic of discussion, especially in recent years, when, with increasing globalization, the volume of international trade grew substantially and financial relations deepened.

Consider the exchange rate between US dollars and Chilean pesos. An exchange rate of 650 means that 650 Chilean pesos are needed to buy one dollar. If, for example, the exchange rate rises to 680, then the peso has lost value in relation to the dollar and is said to have "depreciated," since more pesos are required to buy the same amount of dollars.

In an open economy, the price levels of different countries are connected by the exchange rate. Suppose a laptop costs $1,000 dollars in the United States. If transportation costs and import tariffs are ignored, and if we consider that at the beginning of 2018, approximately 20 Argentinian pesos were equivalent to a US dollar, the price of this machine in Argentina would be approximately 20,000 pesos. In general terms, if the goods produced in two countries are traded freely, their prices are related through the market exchange rate. This is known as the *law of one price*. *Purchasing power parity* (PPP), as was explained in the first chapter, extends the law of one price to a basket of goods and services and states that the price levels of the same basket of goods in two countries (or regions) are related through the exchange rate.

While in a closed economy, increases in the money supply generate an increase in the price level, the result in an open economy depends on the exchange rate regime that the country has chosen. Today one can see a wide variety of exchange rate regimes, which in simple terms may be classified into fixed and flexible exchange rate systems.

Fixed Exchange Rate System

In a *fixed exchange rate* system, the central bank of a country commits to buying and selling foreign currency at a fixed price. In other words, the central bank commits to exchanging foreign currency for local currency at a certain exchange rate value. Let's say, for instance, in the case of the Argentinian peso, if the exchange rate were fixed at 20 pesos per dollar, then every time a foreigner arrived in Argentina with $100 in need of local currency, he or she would receive 2,000 pesos in return. A fixed exchange rate implies that the monetary authority must regulate whatever excesses of foreign currency may exist to keep the value of the exchange rate at the level it committed to. This means that under fixed exchange rates, a country loses partial (or total) control of its money supply since any increase or decrease in the amount of money is governed by an increase or decrease in the international reserves kept by the central bank. By losing control of its money supply, the monetary authority is now unable to provide liquidity to the banking system, as we saw in the previous section.

An example of this system is the currency board, which Argentina had until the end of 2001 and Hong Kong has to this day. In such a scheme the local currency is pegged to a foreign currency (typically the US dollar or the euro) at a fixed rate. This type of system maintains absolute and unlimited convertibility (at a fixed value) between its notes and coins and the currency against which it is pegged and requires that the currency board's foreign currency reserves be sufficient to ensure that all holders of its notes and coins can convert them. Currently, countries such as Hong Kong (pegged to the US dollar) and Estonia (pegged to the euro) use this kind of scheme.

Another, more radical option is to directly use the currency of another country. For example, El Salvador, Ecuador, and Panama "dollarized" by switching their official local currency to US dollars. This is a totally fixed exchange rate system because it fixes the value of local goods and services to the value of the US dollar. Within a monetary union—such as the euro zone—the member countries share a currency, which is equivalent to adopting an irrevocably fixed exchange rate among them. Under this regime, the currency used is regulated by a common authority (in this case, the ECB) that watches over the interests of the whole area. But what happens if member countries require different monetary policies? This question highlights the difficulty of belonging to a monetary union, as was the case in Europe during the subprime mortgage crisis. In mid-2011 the ECB decided to raise the interest rate, arguing that the recovery part of Europe was experiencing justified a normalization of monetary policy and ensuring that average inflation in the region would be kept at bay. By this time, other countries in the euro zone, such as Spain and Greece, were in a deep crisis and needed lower rates and greater aid to facilitate their recovery. Finally the ECB reversed the measure, again lowering interest rates at the end of 2011 and making massive injections of liquidity through several programs in the euro zone.

A country with a fixed exchange rate, whether it is fixed by a currency board or through the simple commitment of the authority to maintaining a fixed parity, can face the dilemma of floating (i.e., adopting a flexible scheme in which the currency price is set by the money market based on supply and demand; we explain this in more detail in the next section) or dollarizing. Each option involves both costs and benefits. Argentina faced such a dilemma between 2001 and 2002 because of the lack of credibility regarding its ability to maintain the convertibility scheme. The sustenance of a currency board relies on the compliance of a series of requirements to ensure the *real* value (or market value) of the currency is equivalent to the peg. However, Argentina did not meet these standards, which made the currency board lose credibility. The market did not believe the currency was actually worth what the Argentinean monetary authority had pegged it to. And when the market consistently bets against a currency, it can force a devaluation and a change of exchange rate regime.

What leads a country to give up its currency? Dollarization eliminates (or dramatically decreases) uncertainty regarding the future level of the exchange rate. Reducing or eliminating this uncertainty will lower interest rates, reducing the cost of public and private borrowing. Additional benefits of dollarization (or *euroization*, or other such schemes) include the convergence toward the inflation rate of the country whose currency is used, lower transaction costs in the country, and trade facilitation. However, this option completely abolishes the monetary policy instrument, which prevents the country from responding to internal shocks (droughts, floods) or external shocks (a fall in export prices, an international financial panic) by reducing interest rates or allowing for the depreciation of the currency.

Flexible Exchange Rate System

The flexible exchange rate system lies at the other extreme of the spectrum: it allows buffering of external shocks and the use of monetary policy to manage the money supply. This enables the central bank to help the banking system when it faces a possible crisis, for example. However, under this scheme, exaggerated increases in the money supply translate into a strong depreciation of the exchange rate and, consequently, higher inflation rates.

To keep inflation under control in a floating rate system, it is critical that the central bank be an autonomous entity and that it set explicit inflation targets, as in Chile, Colombia, Mexico, and Peru. Inflation targets, whether they are specific-value targets or within a target range, help create a predictable environment for decision-making by informing economic agents in advance of the path that is intended for monetary policy. At the same time, these targets must be credible. Credibility, though not easily obtained, can be gradually acquired through macroeconomic responsibility, particularly on the part of the monetary authority. This is most easily achieved when the central bank is independent of the government and hence able to resist pressure from the government to print money or finance fiscal deficits.

To see how the exchange rate is related to the financial market, let us look at the simple example shown in figure 4. Suppose we were deciding between investing some of

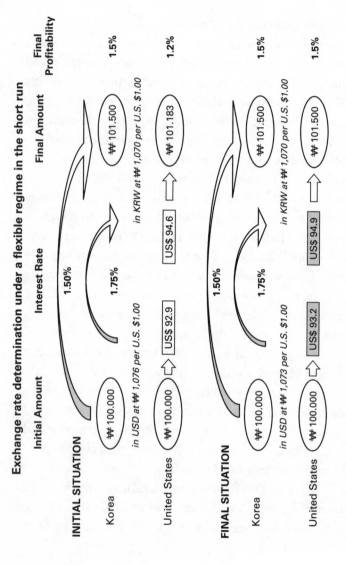

Figure 4 Determination of the exchange rate in the short term in a flexible exchange rate system.

our money in Korea or in the United States. If we invest ₩100,000 in Korea, at the current level of rates we would have $101,500 by the end of the year, which implies a return of 1.5 percent (101,500/100,000 − 1). If we decide to invest in the United States, we would first have to change our money into dollars, which at an exchange rate of ₩1,076 per dollar would be equivalent to US $92.9. With the US interest rate at 1.75 percent, the investment would return US $94.60 after a year. The profitability of these alternatives must be compared using a common currency, which calls for an additional conversion of those dollars to won. The problem is that we do not know for certain what the value of the dollar will be in a year, but let us suppose that certain financial transactions (called "forward" or "future" operations) indicate that we can buy or sell foreign currency a year from now at a known rate, say ₩1,070 per dollar. If this proves to be the case, the $94.60 would be ₩101,183. Hence investing in the United States would have a rate of return of 1.2 percent. Apparently, then, it would be more profitable to invest the $100,000 in Korea.

However, the story does not end there. Those people who have their money in the United States will try to invest it in Korea because of the greater profitability of the investment. As these investments are made, the exchange rate will gradually fall because the dollar becomes less desirable than the Korean won; thus the won appreciates and the dollar depreciates. This will happen until the exchange rate stabilizes at ₩1,073 per dollar. Why? Because at this value, investing in the United States and investing in Korea will be equally attractive, and no one will have an incentive to transfer money between one country and the other. In this way the differences in returns in the financial markets determine the exchange rate in the short term.

The Debate over Exchange Rate Systems

What is the difference between adopting one or the other exchange rate regime? To answer this question, it is useful to analyze the reaction of a small country to a fall in the price of its exports. Suppose exports are concentrated in raw materials, such as copper in Chile and Peru, oil in Nigeria, Venezuela, and Ecuador, and oil and coffee in Colombia.

Consider Colombia. What if, for some reason, the world price of coffee dropped? First, export earnings would decrease, and therefore the overall income of Colombians would fall. In economies that are highly integrated (commercially and financially) with the rest of the world, such a drop would have a small effect on consumption, because, as will be seen in chapters 7 and 9, the drop in national income would be compensated by greater borrowing from other countries, meaning that overall consumption of the inhabitants of that country could remain almost the same.

However, some economies with a high level of previous debt have limited borrowing capacity, and therefore they are unlikely to obtain more financial resources to compensate for a drop in their income (as in the example).

Additionally, suppose that the physical volume of coffee exported remained unchanged. As fewer dollars would be entering the country for the same exported volume, dollars would be scarcer, and therefore the exchange rate would tend to rise. With a flexible exchange rate scheme, the Colombian peso would depreciate and Colombian exports would be more competitive. This would promote an increase in noncoffee exports, which would in turn help restore global economic activity and thus offset the decline in the price of coffee.

What would happen if the exchange rate was fixed? Think of an extreme case, like that of Ecuador, which currently uses the dollar for its transactions. If oil prices fell, the Central Bank of Ecuador would have to adopt a policy to reduce consumption and investment without being able to use the exchange rate because the exchange rate is irrevocably fixed. This would generate much more unemployment than a flexible exchange rate; higher unemployment would tend to reduce wages and prices to regain external competitiveness.

But, as many countries' experiences have demonstrated, there is great resistance from workers to accepting a reduction in wages and from shops to lowering their prices. In such a case, the adjustment becomes slower and more painful, as it will require a long period of high unemployment and low levels of sales before the economy recovers to the level of activity before the shock.

Already in the 1950s, Nobel laureate Milton Friedman advocated using a flexible exchange rate system. Recent economic research tends to support Friedman's proposal.

FISCAL DEFICITS, INFLATION, AND EXTERNAL CRISES

This chapter examines the effects of the fiscal deficit under fixed and flexible exchange rate regimes, the balance of payments crises in Mexico, Argentina, and Southeast Asia, and the causes of the subprime crisis in the United States and its subsequent spread to the euro area.

Fiscal Deficits under Fixed and Flexible Exchange Rate Regimes

If a country adopts a fixed exchange rate regime, the fiscal deficit financed by issuing money will result in a loss of international reserves. This happens because, as people begin to have more money than they need for their transactions, they try to invest in other financial alternatives, some of them abroad. To do so, investors first need to convert domestic money into foreign currency, but when they do, the exchange rate tends to depreciate.

To keep the local currency from depreciating (i.e., to maintain the exchange rate), the central bank needs to intervene, selling reserves. Therefore, if reserves are available, the exchange rate will be able to remain fixed, and the country will avoid inflation. However, if the deficit persists and reserves are depleted, the central bank will have no choice but to devalue its currency—or let the exchange rate float, changing from a fixed system to a flexible one. Ultimately, it will not be possible to avoid inflation.

With a free or floating exchange rate system, a persistent deficit is also directly financed through monetary issuance. However, since in this case the central bank does not undertake actions to maintain the exchange rate, it will continuously depreciate. This will increase domestic prices, especially the prices of those goods that are tradable internationally, such as export goods, and those that are imported or substitute imports.

In the end, the fiscal deficit will lead to higher inflation rates. This is equivalent to financing the deficit with a tax—the inflation tax—that the government "charges" those who keep national currency as cash or in their bank accounts. In other words, since financing fiscal deficits by issuing money leads to a higher inflation rate, this sort of financing will result in a reduction of the value of the national currency maintained by the public. From a governmental point of view, such a tax has the advantage of not needing legislative approval or requiring further administrative costs for its application. However, it is an inefficient and regressive tax, since inflation affects those who have the least to a greater extent than those who have more. This is because the poor, having less chance of saving and keeping their money in the bank or in assets that are protected from inflation (as those of higher means do), generally keep a greater proportion of their money as cash. By doing so, they also pay a greater proportion of their income as inflation tax than those who have higher income. This is what we mean when we say that an inflation tax is a very regressive tax.

The Chilean experience between 1970 and 1973 illustrates the relationship between fiscal deficit, loss of reserves, and inflation. During this period, the government increased expenditure (to stimulate the economy) and, because the central bank was not independent (recall the importance of an autonomous central bank, discussed in the previous chapter), public spending was almost completely financed by monetary issuance by the central bank. The public sector deficit went from a little more than 6 percent of GDP to an astronomical 30 percent of GDP. Meanwhile, and unsurprisingly, inflation shot up and shortages deepened as a result of price controls and restrictions on international trade. Eventually, in an effort to keep inflation under control and somehow compensate for the cost of this growing fiscal deficit, international reserves kept by the central bank fell from 41 percent to 9 percent of annual imports. Other similar situations occurred in Peru between 1985 and 1988, during the populist government of Alan García, and in Argentina between 2001 and 2002. In the case of Argentina, the fall in international reserves was less pronounced as a result of help from international organizations such as the International Monetary Fund (IMF). The three cases of Chile, Peru, and Argentina deliver a similar lesson: a high and growing fiscal expenditure and fiscal deficit that are financed with the issuance of money cannot coexist with a fixed exchange rate. In the end, they are financed by a loss of international reserves, and the deficit becomes unsustainable.

Balance of Payments Crisis

The collapse of a fixed exchange rate regime is a *balance of payments crisis*, which occurs when the central bank faces a progressive depletion of its international reserves and is forced to give up the fixed exchange rate. If the public anticipates such a collapse, individuals who own national money will be quick to exchange it for foreign currency, usually US dollars. This phenomenon is known as a *speculative attack*, which depletes the foreign currency reserves of the central bank or takes them to a minimum level.

Mexico, 1994–1995

A good example of a balance of payments collapse was Mexico in late 1994 and early 1995. In contrast to the recurring crises in Argentina, which were mainly due to excessive spending in the public sector, Mexico's problems did not originate in a large fiscal deficit (in fact, the budget was almost in balance) but rather in an unusual expansion of private spending, fueled by a credit boom.

Central bank reserves exceeded $20 billion for most of 1993 and peaked at $29 billion in March 1994, partly because of Mexico's integration with the United States and Canada in the *North American Free Trade Agreement (NAFTA)* in January 1994. At that time, Mexico was also going through the last stages of applying for membership in the Organisation for Economic Co-operation and Development (OECD).

The economic reforms of the previous decade induced a low rate of inflation and a reduction of the fiscal deficit. These economic conditions, coupled with Mexico's increased international openness and favorable position in the international financial markets, contributed to the high levels of capital inflows into the country in the early 1990s.

However, in the second quarter of 1994, US interest rates began to rise. This, added to the assassination of presidential candidate Luis Donaldo Colosio in March 1994 and the armed revolt in Chiapas, abruptly stopped capital inflows into Mexico. Mexican Central Bank reserves began to decline and continued to fall throughout the year. The central bank maintained the exchange parity, but in doing so it depleted its reserves. In December of that year reserves reached $5 billion ($24 billion less than in February); at that point the authorities were forced to let the exchange rate float.

Thus a wave of financial panic broke out and investors quickly took their assets out of the country. Foreign markets refused to grant new loans to the Mexican government, and the country was about to declare a suspension in the payment of its debts in dollars (a moratorium). However, Mexico was able avoid this with the help of the United States and the IMF through a huge emergency loan. *Foreign currency reserves* were already at $4 billion in January 1995 and the exchange rate, which in November was trading at around 3.4 pesos per US dollar, reached almost 7 pesos per dollar in March. Despite the international rescue operation, the year 1995 marked a deep recession in Mexico, which showed that a financial crisis is very costly to the real economy.

Argentina's Crises

Another example of a balance of payments crisis, although with even more painful nuances, occurred in Argentina between 2001 and 2002, when the currency board (a fixed exchange rate scheme set by law) in force since the early 1990s collapsed. During the first half of 2001 central bank reserves had remained stable at around $24 billion.

However, three continuous years of recession, high rates of tax evasion, and government reluctance to lower levels of public spending made the fiscal deficit uncontrollable. This explains the fact that between July and August of that year, international reserves diminished by $6.5 billion—almost a third of their initial value. An IMF bailout program in September resulted in reserves rebounding to $21 billion and allowed the fixed exchange rate system to continue.

Sadly, confidence in the economic program soon faded. The country was unable to resort to external financing (or issuing government debt to international investors) because the country risk premium was fifteen percentage points higher than a US treasury bond, a level of risk that was unacceptable to most investors. The country also faced prohibitive costs for internal borrowing (or issuing government debt to national investors) as the country risk premium skyrocketed. This reflected the fact that government debt had become a very risky investment to make and therefore very costly for the government to pay back to investors. As a result, the authorities initially met the increasing demand for foreign currency by selling the country's reserves at an average rate of $400 million per month.

In December 2001 the situation became critical, and restrictions on financial operations were tightened to avoid a massive speculative attack. Thus the financial *corralito* was established to prevent people from withdrawing their funds deposited in the banking system. This led to a series of social conflicts that resulted in the fall of President Fernando de la Rúa.

After a period of political uncertainty, reflected in the unprecedented record of having five presidents in less than two weeks, the administration of President Eduardo Duhalde chose to devalue the exchange rate until it reached 1.4 pesos per dollar, as a way of preserving international reserves, in the hope that a controlled devaluation would prevent inflation from spiraling. However, a few months later, a flexible exchange rate system was adopted and the peso devalued by about 200 percent against the dollar; annual inflation exceeded 40 percent.

This phenomenon, however, was not new for Argentina. At the end of the 1980s something similar had happened during the administration of President Raúl Alfonsín, when the so-called Austral Plan collapsed. And more recently, in 2011, during the administration of Cristina Fernández de Kirchner, the exchange rate was again relatively fixed under a policy of strict capital controls; inflation began to rise, nonetheless, in the face of the expectation that further depreciation would be inevitable. Currency liberalization (a flexible exchange rate system) materialized a few years later with the arrival of President Mauricio Macri at the end of 2015; Macri had to bear the economic costs of depreciation and corrective inflation.

Argentine's repeated experience illustrates that when a fixed exchange rate system is forced with no fiscal discipline, a balance of payments crisis is almost inevitable.

The Contrasts of the Asian Crisis of 1997–1998

The Southeast *Asian crisis* in the second half of the 1990s is another example of a balance of payments crisis. However, an important distinction must be made. The role of the state in the Asian crisis is different from that in the South American cases presented above because in the Asian case there were no unsustainable fiscal deficits. In the words of Paul Krugman of Princeton University, the Asian crisis was much less a "balance of payments crisis" than a "bad banking crisis," in the sense that the usual model used by economists to analyze phenomena of this type (governments with high deficits + inflexible currencies = loss of reserves + crisis) was insufficient when attempting to explain the fall of the *Asian tigers*. The so-called Asian tigers are four economies—Hong Kong, Singapore, South Korea, and Taiwan—that underwent a rapid industrialization process and maintained exceptionally high growth rates between the early 1960s and the 1990s.

In July 1997, the Thai currency (baht) was devalued, contradicting repeated statements by government authorities that this would not happen. In a matter of days the currencies of Indonesia, the Philippines, and Malaysia faced speculative attacks; that is, people in those countries exchanged their local currency for foreign currency in high volumes, causing the local currency to collapse. By the end of October the South Korean won had collapsed, and the crisis spread across Asia.

Paradoxically, just a few months before the crises, not only did analysts see these economies as solid and stable, but these countries were looked up to by the international financial community. And yet most East Asian economies suffered a severe recession in 1998. How could a region that had been so successful experience such a sudden and severe collapse?

The increase in capital inflows into emerging markets during the first half of the 1990s generated large volumes of new investment but at the same time resulted in the loss of competitiveness of Asian currencies that operated under fixed exchange rate regimes. At the beginning of 1997 at least two currencies, the Thai baht and the Korean won, appeared ready for devaluation. Domestic and foreign investors began to convert part of their local currency reserves into foreign currency. This caused a gradual loss of international reserves. As a result, the Central Bank of Thailand was forced to devalue on July 2, 1997.

Many Asian banks had large short-term dollar-denominated debts with international investors, especially with international banks in Europe, the United States, and Japan. When the Thai currency was devalued, investors accelerated the withdrawal of their loans from the region, fearing that if they did not do so, much of the short-term debt would remain unpaid. Asian banks were not able to easily repay their external creditors as they had money placed in loans for long-term investment projects such as factories and real estate. Such banks could not simply repay the volume of short-term loans that were coming due.

The possibility of default increased, and the sense of an imminent chaos aggravated the panic among external creditors. Many debtors were bankrupted, and Asian currencies began to crumble as investors, both domestic and foreign, sought to withdraw their funds from the region as soon as possible. When one of the countries fell prey to panic, neighboring countries, in addition to dealing with their own problems, had to face the problems that arose from *contagion*.

The Phenomenon of Contagion: From the Russian Crisis to the Brazilian Crisis

Globalization, which is discussed in greater detail in chapter 11, has brought enormous benefits, but also carries risks. With the passage of time, countries have become increasingly linked, especially through trade and capital movements. In this way, a country-specific shock can be quickly transmitted to others. This has generated the need to incorporate the analysis of contagion into the study of crises.

However, it is not enough to consider contagion as a key element of crises. Globalization has also required rethinking the way in which this phenomenon was traditionally conceived. In analyzing contagion, the impact of a country's crisis on geographically contiguous countries was usually emphasized. In fact, the studies that dealt with the subject considered that in those countries belonging to the same region as the country in crisis, the perception of risk by investors increased, which led to capital flight, precipitating the collapse of the exchange rate and therefore validating their expectations.

The Russian crisis showed that this view of contagion was insufficient. By 1998 Russia had a rather large fiscal deficit, as well as a growing public debt. On the other hand, the prices of its export products dropped severely. The situation was aggravated by the impact of the Asian crisis on Russia. Investors' confidence quickly plummeted, and they began liquidating their ruble assets and buying foreign currencies. In August of that year, capital outflows from the country increased, and as a result, the government was forced to declare bankruptcy and later to let the exchange rate float. Panic took over the markets, and

With the passage of time, countries have become increasingly linked, especially through trade and capital movements.

investors began fleeing emerging economies, fearing that such a situation would also occur in other countries, especially those whose economic fundamentals had deteriorated and which were thus more exposed to a crisis. Thus the next link in the chain was Brazil, which had a considerable current account deficit (a situation in which the value of the country's imports is greater than the value of its exports and transfers from the rest of the world), as well as a large public debt. After the outbreak of the Russian crisis, capital began to flee the Brazilian economy, such that the central bank continually lost international reserves until it finally had no choice but to let the exchange rate float. That started the Brazilian crisis, which expanded to the rest of the Latin American countries and especially to Argentina.

The contagion of Brazil surprised many analysts since Russia at that time represented barely more than 1 percent of world output, while its trade with the emerging economies was quantitatively unimportant. Since trade channels had practically no relevance in this episode, this indicates that contagion occurred mainly through financial channels. In fact, there is evidence that the contagion was triggered by foreign investors panicking with the Russian crisis, which also led them to speculate against the currencies of other large developing markets, such as Brazil. This had little to do with trade flows among countries and much more to do with the interconnection of the global financial system. Since then, it has become standard to distinguish between regional and global contagion. The contagion of Russia to Brazil can only be explained as global, whereas the effects of the fall of Brazil, transmitted to the rest of Latin America, are framed within the traditional form of regional contagion, in which commercial links are much more relevant, since Brazil is an important trading partner for several Latin American countries.

The Subprime Crisis, 2008–2009

The *subprime mortgage crisis*, which originated in the United States and rapidly globalized, is a more general case of an *external crisis* than the previous ones. In the first place, it covered both countries with a fixed exchange rate and those with a floating rate. Second, the resulting recession has been the deepest of the postwar period, although far from the Great Depression of the 1930s. Here we analyze its origins and development.

The recession that occurred between March and November of 2001, together with the attacks of September 11 of that year, generated an enormous climate of instability that ended up setting the stage for the US Federal Reserve to start a strong expansionary cycle in its monetary policy. In effect, the policy interest rate (the monetary policy rate discussed in the previous chapter) fell from 6.5

percent at the end of 2000 to 1 percent in mid-2003. As a result, large sums of money were invested in the real estate sector. Initially the boom in the sector manifested itself in high growth rates of housing sales and house prices, among other indicators.

The environment of high liquidity allowed credit to be extended to low-income clients or to people without fixed employment or lacking other assets to back their loans. Mortgages used for the purchase of housing by this group of clients are known as subprime mortgages and are associated with a higher risk of default than prime mortgages. However, the US economy was recovering rapidly from the 2001 recession, making it easier for debtors to find work and pay off their loans. At the same time, investors took advantage of the increase in housing prices, initiating greater speculative transactions that fueled the boom. Homeowners felt richer, as the value of their real estate multiplied with respect to their acquisition value, increasing their wealth and allowing them to raise their consumption level.

On the other hand, some countries had huge amounts of savings, especially those with high current account surpluses, such as China and the oil-exporting countries. Strong investor demand for assets with higher returns led to the creation of new financial products. This so-called financial engineering generated products such as *collateralized debt obligations* (CDOs), which assembled a combination of different types of loans and other financial assets, to diversify risk and obtain good ratings from risk rating agencies. In other words, risky subprime mortgages were bundled with other, safer loans and sold to investors. Investors would make profits when the loans were repaid. Banks began selling their loans (including subprime mortgages) to institutions that created CDOs, which in turn sold them to mutual funds. Once this happened, it was no longer possible to identify who had assumed the original risk. As the increased risk was sold to a third party, banks entered the subprime market with greater force.

However, the situation began to change as of 2004. Inflation accelerated to levels undesired by the Federal Reserve, and so the Fed began a restrictive monetary policy to control it. The rate rose from 1 percent to 5.25 percent between mid-2004 and 2006, which caused a consequent increase in mortgage interest rates. Debt defaults started to rise sharply, triggering a wave of foreclosures, and the real estate market started to contract. In early 2006, housing sales began to drop, and, while prices continued to increase, they did so at a much slower rate than in the previous few years.

Some thought that the contraction was limited to the real estate market. However, as noted earlier, major financial institutions such as banks and mutual funds had a portfolio of assets heavily reliant on subprime mortgages. The portfolio of overdue mortgages reached a critical level, after which the CDOs began to depreciate, and holders realized that the risk had not been properly evaluated. This forced the holders of these assets to sell other assets to offset their losses, generating a massive liquidation of risky assets. In mid-2007 several investment funds began to succumb, and various financial companies broke down. This generated a spiral of mistrust, drastically reducing credit (a *credit crunch*), which in turn led to a liquidity crisis, and the problem spread to the entire economy. Foreclosures continued and residential investment continued to contract, eventually leading housing prices to go from slowdown to contraction. Falling home prices exacerbated the problem, causing losses for homeowners and further diminishing the value of subprime mortgage assets, which badly deteriorated the banks' portfolios. Things got critical because the lower prices of housing made individuals feel poorer, thus reducing consumption and worsening the economic situation globally.

As of September 2007, the Fed had no alternative but to initiate a drastic reduction in the cost of money, lowering the policy rate from 5.25 percent to 2 percent in April 2008, when there was a pause in its expansionary policy of some months, as it was thought that the economy, although it was undergoing a strong slowdown, could still avoid recession. However, the bankruptcy of investment bank Lehman Brothers in September further collapsed expectations, and the Fed reduced the rate to an unprecedented range of 0 percent to 0.25 percent. Such a low interest rate implies that loans are cheap (almost "free" of interest) and deposits in savings accounts have an extremely low return (making savings accounts largely unattractive). In other words, low interest rates stimulate consumption in the present and discourage saving. Stock markets suffered drastic declines, and panic gripped the markets. The Dow Jones Industrial Average index lost more than 60 percent of its value from its peak to its lowest value after the crisis in March 2009. It was at this stage that the strongest effects of the shift from the financial crisis to the real sector were felt, while the world was facing the worst crisis since the Great Depression.

Thus the world economy had very bad moments between the last quarter of 2008 and the second quarter of 2009, but already in the third quarter of 2009 it was in a strong recovery. This recovery was led by China, other countries of emerging Asia, and Brazil (Latin America), although Brazil would later fall into a deep economic crisis.

The lessons of this crisis have been multiple. Excessively permissive regulations and regulators' controls failed. Risk rating agencies failed, as did many external audits. Incentives for executives led them to take huge risks to be able to exercise their stock options with big profits; those bets also failed.

In summary, crises originating in the financial sector follow certain similar characteristics, and the subprime crisis was no exception. In the lead-up to a crisis, there is an expansion of credit, a feeling of greater wealth, and a willingness to take bigger risks, which leads to sharp increases in indebtedness. These symptoms are usually ignored by the marketplace, which is known as the syndrome of "this time is different." When people realize that the possibility of a crisis is real, panic spreads among investors, who quickly sell their assets. The consequent decline in asset prices, in a context of high indebtedness, leads to the collapse of the economic system.

As was the case during the Southeast Asian crisis, in a world interconnected by international trade and financial flows, contagion effects on other economies can be very relevant. The repercussions of the subprime crisis were not expected in the rest of the world. While Latin America and the emerging world managed to rebound quickly, the effects of the crisis hit the euro area particularly hard, with some member countries accumulating major fiscal imbalances.

The Euro Crisis, 2010–2011

To analyze the euro crisis, it is necessary to understand that a common currency is technically a fixed exchange rate regime. By joining the euro, member countries give up the possibility of adjusting their exchange rate, and monetary policy remains in the hands of a common entity for the whole area, the European Central Bank (ECB).

During the years leading up to the subprime crisis, Europe experienced extremely favorable conditions, with access to international financing at very low interest rates. This led countries such as Spain, Greece, and Portugal to experience strong expansions of their domestic spending, both public and private, accumulating important deficits in their current account that ranged between 10 percent and 15 percent of GDP in 2009. This contrasts with the case of Germany, which kept its fiscal accounts in balance during the period.

The excess of spending in these countries led to a deterioration in their competitiveness, as the price of local goods became more expensive in relation to tradable goods, while at the same time asset prices increased massively. With the explosion of the subprime crisis, international interest rates began to rise, and these countries lost access to the cheap financing that had sustained their excess spending in the recent past. Domestic spending contracted sharply, with immediate effects on public accounts, unemployment, and the solvency of the banks.

A first problem faced by European countries in crisis was that, being part of a monetary union, they could not resort to depreciating their exchange rates to make their exports more competitive and stimulate the economy through the external sector. The picture was even more complex insofar as different European countries lived very dissimilar realities. While unemployment was low in Germany, in Portugal it stood at over 15 percent, and in Spain and Greece it was as high as 25 percent. Thus, while Germany was concerned that inflation would return to the ECB's target of close to 2 percent, countries in crisis were calling for interest rate cuts to stimulate their economies.

Monetary unions require that member countries have a certain level of convergence so that a common monetary policy can be applied to all of them. However, the high indebtedness and fiscal imbalances of some countries in the euro zone made such convergence impossible. Although the agreement imposed some fiscal discipline on countries, the maintenance of relatively low and stable inflation figures led the authorities to complacency with countries that exceeded the established limits on fiscal deficits. In this way, the actions of the monetary authority were initially hesitant until the magnitude of the crisis made inevitable a drastic lowering of rates, which were kept close to 0 percent for several years, and the financing of large rescue packages for troubled countries. In addition, the ECB initiated unorthodox packages of monetary expansion in March 2015, including quantitative easing (QE, a nonconventional monetary policy measure discussed in chapter 4), which led to massive increases in the monetary base. As in the case of the United States, QE measures in the euro zone sought to reactivate the economy mainly by buying bonds (or debt) from commercial banks, allowing them to refinance themselves at lower interest rates. Basically, the ECB bought bonds from banks, increasing the price of these bonds and creating money in the banking system. This caused interest rates to fall, making loans cheaper. Businesses and people were then able to borrow more and spend less to repay their debts. By reactivating consumption and investment, the ECB's actions also facilitated economic growth and job creation.

To sum up, the causes of the euro crisis were a combination of factors whose mechanics were not much different from those in the cases discussed previously. An excessive increase in domestic spending, in this case both public and private, led to an accumulation of deficits that became unsustainable when international conditions changed because of the subprime crisis. On the other hand, the impossibility of resorting to a currency depreciation when belonging to a monetary union limited the maneuvers available to these countries to stimulate their economy.

THE ECONOMIC COST
OF STABILIZING INFLATION

What are the problems associated with high rates of inflation? Why have industrialized countries and the more dynamic economies of Asia consistently had lower inflation than Latin American countries? Why did global inflation rise strongly in 2008, then drop sharply in 2009? Are there any costs associated with this process? This chapter addresses these and other issues.

To understand the historical context, it is necessary to go back to the 1970s and 1980s, when a heated debate in academic circles arose about the least expensive way to stop inflation, as this phenomenon appeared with an unusual force, stimulated by the sharp rise in the price of oil in 1973 and high fiscal deficits.

The main controversy was not whether inflation should be reduced but how and at what speed. Many thought that a rapid fall in inflation could only be achieved by inducing a recession, using restrictive monetary and fiscal policies. The other alternative was to gradually reduce inflation through a mild economic slowdown, though at the cost of accepting the undesirable consequences of inflation for a longer time. In the United States, the Reagan administration opted for the first of these two options in 1981. The immediate costs of this decision were evident: a 2 percent drop in GDP in 1982 and an increase in unemployment to almost 10 percent. However, not only were there immediate benefits, with inflation dropping from 10.3 percent in 1981 to 3.2 percent in 1983, but what seemed to have been negatively affected by the "Reagan Revolution" revealed positive results in the medium term. GDP growth rates picked up in the following years to 4.6 percent in 1983, 7.3 percent in 1984, and 4.2 percent in 1985, and the unemployment rate also fell from almost 10 percent to 7.5 percent in 1984, 7.2 percent in 1985, and 7 percent in 1986. The United States' inflation rate has exceeded 5 percent only once in the last two decades, thanks in great part to the performance of the Federal Reserve.

An example of the alternative and gradual way of reducing inflation can be seen in Chile, where in 1990 inflation reached 27.3 percent and nine years later had fallen to 2.3 percent. The stabilization process occurred simultaneously with the creation of an autonomous central bank. In fact, an important part of the credit for stabilization should be attributed to this institutional reform, which adopted an inflation-targeting scheme in that period, an approach that gained high credibility in the market.

Nonstabilization without Reducing Fiscal Deficits

It should be clear that in general, the primary cause of high inflation is a high and sustained fiscal deficit. Unless that problem is solved, inflation will reappear every time, like a Phoenix rising from its ashes.

Since the well-known works of Thomas Sargent, macroeconomic theory has recognized that a government running persisting deficits will need, sooner or later, to finance those deficits by issuing money. Normally, a government would finance its deficit by borrowing abroad, borrowing from local financial institutions, or selling public assets accumulated in previous periods. However, after successive periods of high fiscal deficits, the government will have accumulated meaningful liabilities, its public assets will be depleted, and its payment capacity will appear questionable to foreign and local investors. If a country's ability to repay debt is doubted by investors, external financing will no longer be an option to finance its deficit, or rather, it would have to be done at excessively high rates. This situation would most likely lead to pressuring the central bank (or monetary authority) to finance the government's deficit.

The central bank can finance the fiscal deficit in several ways, such as by making cash advances to the public or by purchasing public bonds. In any case, these mechanisms imply a continuous emission of money, which will eventually translate into higher inflation rates. When the monetary authority (such as a central bank) is not completely autonomous from the government, scenarios such as these are more likely.

The close relationship between fiscal deficits and inflation has been well documented empirically, especially in developing economies. A recent example is that of Argentina. The Macri administration inherited a large fiscal deficit of 5.7 percent of GDP in 2015, after seven years of successive deficits. The Argentine government adopted a gradual approach and the fiscal deficit continued to grow, but at slower rates: 6.3 percent in 2016 and 6.4 percent in 2017. With this, inflation declined slowly from 36 percent in 2016 to 25 percent in 2017. While the deficit persisted, however, it was mainly financed by printing money, which fueled inflation.

Credibility and the Autonomy of the Central Bank

Moreover, as we learned in previous chapters, *central bank autonomy* is fundamental for ensuring overall economic stability, especially in terms of inflation.

It is essential that the private sector feel confident that the authorities take seriously the control of inflation. The more serious the effort is perceived to be, the faster inflation expectations will adjust and the easier it will be to achieve the target. If the central bank can create clear rules—such as publicly announcing its inflation targets—then, by associating them with its own policy instruments, it will increase the credibility of the anti-inflationary program, thus helping to reduce the costs of stabilization.

In some countries, when people perceive that the central bank is subordinated to political power, confidence in that institution is greatly diminished. So, to strengthen the credibility of the central bank, many countries have separated it from government control and granted it sufficient autonomy to refuse to approve loans to the government. Such a measure has already proved to be very effective when put into practice.

Table 4 shows an indicator of the degree of central bank political independence in nineteen countries between 1991 and 2003, along with their average inflation rate. In this case, central banks are scored from less autonomous (score of 0) to more autonomous (score of 8). The table shows a clear relationship between the degree of autonomy and inflation: the more independent the central bank, the lower is the inflation rate.

Table 4 Central bank autonomy and inflation in different countries

----

Country	Average inflation rate 1991–2003 (%)	Central bank political autonomy score
Japan	0.7	8
France	1.7	8
Switzerland	1.9	8
Austria	2.0	7
Belgium	2.0	8
Germany	2.1	8
New Zealand	2.2	5
Denmark	2.2	8
United Kingdom	2.7	8
United States	2.9	8
Ireland	3.0	4
Italy	3.7	3
Spain	4.0	8
Portugal	5.1	8
Egypt	8.5	5
Greece	8.8	3
Mexico	16.4	1
Zambia	61.1	0

Source: Arnone et al., "Central Bank Autonomy"; International Monetary Fund, *World Economic Outlook 2018.*

The Costs of Inflation

There is a consensus that high and volatile inflation rates are costly for a country's economy. It has come to be thought that if prices and incomes were to rise at the same pace as inflation, there would be no problem. However, even in this case there would be costs associated with inflation.

First, inflation is a tax on the possession of money that does not require legislative approval. As people need money to carry out transactions, they lose part of its value by using it as a means for exchange, because of the mere existence of inflation. Therefore, people try to protect themselves by exchanging local money for goods or foreign currency.

This behavior is characteristic of the most extreme cases of high inflation or hyperinflation, which occurs when the monthly inflation rate exceeds 50 percent. This phenomenon has been observed in several countries: in Germany between 1920 and 1922; Bolivia between 1984 and 1985; Argentina, Brazil, and Peru between 1989 and 1990; and Nicaragua beginning in 1986. Nicaragua had hyperinflation for no less than fifty-eight months in a row, with an average inflation rate of 260 percent per month. Moreover, for some months in 2008 the rate of inflation in Zimbabwe exceeded 11 million percent. The desire to immediately exchange money for goods or foreign currency

Inflation is a tax on the possession of money that does not require legislative approval.

is extremely strong in these cases. At the beginning of 2009 the circulation of other currencies in Zimbabwe began to be allowed, eventually resulting in the dollarization of Zimbabwe's economy, marking a downward turn in the evolution of that country's inflation. Between 2010 and 2013, average inflation was only around 3 percent per annum, and more recently the country has presented negative inflation figures, on the order of minus 2 percent by 2015.

A more recent case of Latin American high inflation is Venezuela, quite illustrative of its social costs. As an oil-dependent economy, this country benefited greatly from the commodity boom during the 2000s, thus sustaining a considerable expansion of public spending from 28 percent of GDP in 1998 to more than 39 percent of GDP in 2006. However, the fall in the price of oil in 2014 had a direct impact on its fiscal accounts, and, as is usual in such situations, Venezuela resorted to monetary issuance to cover the deficit. This led to a sustained increase in inflation, from 21 percent in 2012 to 43 percent in 2013, 57 percent in 2014, 111 percent in 2015, 254 percent in 2016, and more than 1,000 percent in 2017. In 2018, Venezuela had an inflation rate of more than 1 million percent. As a result of the inflationary process, fiscal imbalances, and regulation of foreign trade, Venezuela developed a deep social crisis—in addition to a political and economic crisis—which was reflected in a widespread shortage of basic consumer goods and high poverty rates, among other things.

Inflation also leads to significant redistributions of income and wealth. For example, an individual borrowing in pesos would gain when inflation unexpectedly increased, because in real terms the real value of the debt paid at the end of the loan would be less. Those who are subject to long-term and nominal labor contracts (or with a readjustment clause that underestimates inflation) also experience a loss in real income, as do those who do not have access to financial instruments to protect themselves from inflation, such as foreign currency or inflation-indexed bonds.

Inflation is especially detrimental to the poor. For example, according to the Argentine National Institute of Statistics and Censuses (INDEC), the proportion of poor people rose from 35 percent to 58 percent between September 2001 and October 2002, partly because of the severe economic recession in that country, but especially because of inflation of the value of the basic consumption basket.

Inflation also causes prices to lose their value as providers of information, and usually induces people to make wrong decisions in terms of production and consumption. Thus inflation represents significant costs for the economy, and so a low and more stable inflation rate is best for a country. But how to achieve it? Is there a cost associated with price stabilization in terms of employment and output? To answer these questions, it is first necessary to know the link between such variables.

Inflation and Unemployment

The uncertain relationship between inflation and unemployment has been a constant subject of study for macroeconomists during the last half century.

Is there any reason for the two variables to be related? If there were price flexibility (upward and downward) in all markets and if people had full access to the relevant economic information, no link between inflation and unemployment should be expected. To illustrate this, suppose that the central bank abruptly doubled the amount of money that existed in the economy. In the face of this event, people would have more money to make purchases and would increase their demand for all kinds of goods and services. From the traditional neighborhood store to large shopping centers, sales would grow and prices would start to rise as a way of rationing existing production.

To raise the level of production and sales, entrepreneurs would try to hire more workers, who would gladly accept, though for a higher salary. Under these circumstances, employers would shift wage costs to higher sales prices. At some point prices would be expected to double from their level prior to the monetary expansion, and in the end there would be no impact on economic activity. Thus greater demand does not necessarily imply that production increases.

Moreover, if everyone knew that the central bank had doubled the money supply, it is likely that the price change would be faster than described in the previous paragraph. Prices and wages would quickly double, and this would increase neither employment nor production.

In other circumstances, however, higher demand driven by monetary expansion could be expected to result in increased output and falling unemployment. In the first place, producers may not know for sure whether the higher level of demand they face is the result of increased demand for their products or the result of the central bank's actions to raise the level of activity. In such a case, the central bank may affect output through unforeseen expansionary measures.

Second, there are wage contracts that are typically written for periods of one to three years. As a result, an increase in sales prices would not have as counterpart a higher level of wages. Rather, *real wages* would fall and employers would hire more labor, as discussed in chapter 2. The key elements, then, in determining the relationship between inflation and unemployment, and thus the costs of stabilization, are two: people's expectations and the existence of inflexibilities in wages or prices, such as those resulting from labor contracts.

Inflationary Inertia

Several factors affect the cost of stabilizing inflation, that is, reducing inflation with more or less "pain" in terms of rising unemployment. Such factors determine the degree of inflationary inertia of an economy. The most important are the following:

• *Inflation expectations.* Perhaps nominal wages increase because workers expect an "inflationary surprise." If they do not trust that the government will maintain macroeconomic discipline and readjust their wages upward, foreseeing an increase in the amount of money, inflation will be more difficult to stabilize.

• *Wage indexation.* In some countries, especially those that have gone through long inflationary periods, such as Brazil, nominal wages are automatically adjusted based on past inflation. In the presence of total indexation, if prices increase by 10 percent, wages will be automatically adjusted with a floor of 10 percent. This scheme existed in Chile between 1979 and 1981.

• *Long-term employment contracts.* In such a case, wages are established in contracts that last several years. A three-year contract, for example, may specify that the wage will increase at the beginning of the first, second, and third years. The contract then establishes a nominal wage for each year, which is mainly determined by the expectations of inflation that exist at the time the contract is negotiated.

• *Power of labor negotiation.* Another reason to explain wage increases is the negotiating power of trade unions and other institutions responsible for setting wages.

The higher are inflation expectations, salary indexation, the frequency of labor contracts, and union bargaining power, the greater is the inflationary inertia, and therefore the greater are the employment costs of reducing inflation.

The Sacrifice Coefficient

Once inflation has set in and been incorporated into expectations, there will most likely be a period of higher unemployment to reduce inflation. What is called the "*sacrifice coefficient*" is defined as the excess of unemployment accumulated above its *equilibrium* level (or "natural rate" of unemployment) divided by the reduction of inflation (in percentage points), from the beginning to the end of the stabilization program. In other words, the sacrifice coefficient indicates the cost, in terms of additional unemployment, for each point of reduction in inflation.

Consider as an example the United States' experience in the 1980s. Between 1978 and 1980, US inflation remained persistently in the double digits, a phenomenon not seen for more than half a century. During his presidential campaign of 1980, Ronald Reagan promised emphatically to reduce inflation. To do this, the Federal Reserve (the US Central Bank) used a contractionary monetary policy that caused a recession, although inflation fell from 10.4 percent in 1980 to 3.2 percent in 1984.

What was the cost of stabilization in terms of higher unemployment? The sacrifice coefficient between 1980 and 1984 was calculated using 6 percent as the natural rate of unemployment in the United States. For each year, one must calculate how much unemployment exceeded the natural rate of 6 percent. Between the last quarter of 1980 and the last quarter of 1984, the excess of accumulated unemployment, above the natural rate of 6 percent, was 10.8 percent. From the beginning to the end of the period, inflation fell by 7.2 percent. Thus the sacrifice coefficient was 1.5 (10.8 divided by 7.2), which means that for every one percentage point by which inflation was reduced, unemployment increased by 1.5 percentage points.

Cost Inflation: An Additional Problem of Stabilization

So far we have pointed out that inflation is caused by an increase in the amount of money, which increases the demand for all types of goods and services, pushing prices up. However, this is not always the case. There are times when inflation is not caused by higher demand driven by monetary expansion but rather by an increase in the costs of various productive factors, forcing companies to raise the prices of their products to cope with the increase in costs. This can happen for several reasons. For example, adverse climate conditions or a plague can damage crops, resulting in increased food prices. A sharp increase in oil prices can have a similar effect on goods and services that use it as an input, increasing their prices—as happened twice in the 1970s.

In 2008 the world was affected by *cost inflation*, triggered by rising food and oil prices, and several countries, both developed and emerging, sustained sharp price increases. Note that inflation increased strongly in 2008, but then declined in 2009, along with the prices of those products.

The case of cost inflation is even more complex, since it poses an important dilemma for stabilization. The rise in prices of productive inputs such as oil or wheat carries with it an increase in production costs, which has two effects: a reduction in the use of these inputs to compensate for the increase in costs, which in turn leads to a fall in production and to a partial transfer of the cost increase to the clients. To the degree that inputs such as those mentioned are key elements in the production of other goods and services, this ultimately generates a generalized price increase. As a result, the economy is affected by a slowdown or economic recession coupled with an increase in inflation. Therefore, if the authorities decide to implement a more restrictive monetary policy to combat inflation, this can further aggravate the recession. If the authorities choose to stimulate the economy, there will be high rates of inflation.

The inflationary shock between 2007 and 2008 ended quickly when the international financial crisis broke out in September 2008. When it became clear that there would be a deep contraction of demand in the commodity markets, commodity prices dropped precipitously. World inflation fell during a few months to below 2 percent per year. Therefore, when the crisis broke out, there was no major dilemma for the authorities, as inflation fell, and the authorities of most countries could stimulate the economy without fretting about an escalation in inflation. As a result of the end of the commodity boom, world inflation has had a downward trend after 2013.

THE KEY IMPORTANCE OF
CONSUMPTION AND SAVING

This chapter analyzes the key elements needed to understand the behavior of *consumption*, which basically measures households' expenditures on goods and services that hold no productive purpose for the long term (otherwise such expenditures would be considered an investment). Consumption is fundamental to understanding how an economy works. In fact, it is the main component of GDP, and where most of national production goes.

The Decision between Consumption and Saving

A key question for this analysis is how families determine which part of their *current income* they will save and which part they will consume. Furthermore, how do changes in income and interest rates affect desired levels of consumption and saving at a specific time? To answer such questions, we analyze the origin of the funds that are destined for consumption and saving.

In general, families regularly receive either work income or financial income (income received from financial investments), which adds to the wealth they have inherited or accumulated through time. They additionally have a rough idea of what their future income will be. Hence the decision between consumption and saving depends not only on current income and wealth but also on future expectations. In this sense, perspectives on the future of the economy are key to understanding the behavior leading to the consumption decision.

The following series of events significantly affected consumers in the United States: the beginning of the recession in March 2001; the psychological impact of the attacks of September 11 of that year; the war in Iraq, starting in March 2003; and Hurricane Katrina at the end of August 2005, coupled with a significant increase in inflation. Moreover, consumer indexes were seriously affected by the outbreak of the subprime crisis in August 2007, which led to the beginning of the recession in the United States in late 2007 and, later, in mid-September 2008, to the bankruptcy of Lehman Brothers, which caused widespread panic and a global recession. Likewise, during the run-up to the 2016 presidential elections in the United States, *consumer confidence* was mainly affected by the candidates' encouraging speeches, known as the "honeymoon effect," which historically does not last more than one hundred days after the new government takes office.

Consumer confidence—that is, consumer's expectations about the future—determine their propensity to consume more or less. In other words, both current income and expected future income define the path of consumption over the life of a person, and therefore it is said that consumption and saving decisions are *intertemporal*. In an attempt to maximize their own well-being, families simultaneously decide how much to consume today and how much to consume in the future. They continuously revise the distribution of their present and future consumption according to changes in family income, interest rates, or conditions of access to credit markets.

However, the consumption decision is subject to an important restriction. Although it is true that people can borrow and consume beyond their disposable income for some periods, macroeconomics supposes they cannot spend more than they earn throughout their lives. And, in a way, financial markets guarantee compliance with this restriction. Through the collection of interest, financial institutions make sure that the money they lend will almost certainly be returned by debtors, or else by their family or whoever inherits a debtor's financial duties. Since this is their business, lenders make sure the fraction of issued credit that goes unpaid is as small as possible.

Families prefer a stable consumption path to an unstable one. Since income can fluctuate between periods, the relationship between consumption and current income is not so clear. Families able to borrow money in the financial markets determine their consumption not on the basis of present income but on the basis of *permanent income*. The latter is a kind of average obtained between current income and expected future income.

Macroeconomic theory and evidence show that following a temporary fall in current income, permanent income varies little, consumption does not decrease significantly, and the difference is compensated for with a reduction in saving. However, in the event of a permanent drop in income—also perceived as permanent—consumption decreases by an amount similar to the decrease in income, while saving does not vary much. Hence the consumption path remains relatively stable over time, which has been demonstrated by most empirical studies on the subject.

It is possible to argue that it is not easy to distinguish between a temporary or permanent income variation. In some cases, however, the distinction is not so difficult. Think of the Argentine farmer who grew wheat in the pampas. After a rare drought that affected the United States in 1988, destroying much of that country's wheat crop, the price of grain practically doubled in international markets. The harvest in the pampa was good that year, so the Argentine farmer enjoyed a significant increase in his income when he exported wheat. However, since the drought in the United States was not likely to be repeated in the near future (in light of the country's usual rainfall pattern), the farmer may have done well to consider a good part of his 1988 income as transitory and to save most of his extra income.

Another important observation is that there is a regular pattern of income during a person's lifetime. When people are young, their incomes are low, but because they are likely to earn more over the years, they often become indebted in order to reach their desired consumption level. During their productive years, their income reaches a peak around middle age; they pay off their previous debts and begin saving for retirement. When they retire, their incomes fall, so they must begin to consume the resources they saved until then. One could then divide the life of an average individual into three parts according to saving patterns. Individuals de-save in the first stage, when consumption expenditure is greater than income, by spending their expected future savings; then they save in the second stage, when income is greater than consumption expenditure; and finally they de-save once again in the last stage, when consumption expenditure is again greater than income, by spending savings accumulated in the second stage.

Liquidity Constraints and Precautionary Saving

In general terms, *liquidity constraint* is defined as the inability of some individuals to borrow on the basis of their future income, which is because creditors assume that these individuals will face difficulties in repaying loans and have no guarantee to back a potential loan. This somewhat complicates what we have learned so far about consumption. Moreover, the liquidity constraint means that the assumption that economic agents are able to borrow and lend freely, within the limits imposed by their lifetime income, is not precise, and therefore is no longer valid.

Imagine, for example, a college freshman who believes her prospects for future income are good. If she were to apply for a loan, she might be able to get enough financing to cover all her studies (perhaps thanks to some tax credit), but she will certainly not get enough funds to raise her standard of living to the level of permanent income she expects for the future. Financial markets usually lend against collateral, not just against the promise that a debtor will finance the service of the loan with future earnings.

An important lesson is that, with liquidity constraints, consumption and saving are more closely related to current income than if there were no such restrictions. It is not surprising, then, that in the last forty years, Bolivia's consumption and saving have been closely related to the country's economic growth, as a consequence of the country's low financial development, while in the United States, because of greater financial development and the availability of more financial instruments, the relationship is not as close.

Since consumption depends on expectations about future income, when there is greater uncertainty about the future, people tend to save more. Thus it is reasonable to expect that, of two people with similar average income, the one with a less stable income (say, a farmer) will save more than a person with a more stable income (say, a public employee). This illustrates the phenomenon of *precautionary saving*.

The discussion above helps us understand why, after recessions, consumption reacts cautiously to the recovery of economic activity, even when there are no liquidity constraints. The reason is that people need to be certain whether the negative shock they suffered was of transitory or permanent nature. And, as a result, consumption rises gradually to precrisis levels.

The Chilean experience of the last forty years serves to illustrate the two elements we have just introduced. For much of the country's recent history, GDP and consumption growth were closely related—a clear sign of the presence of liquidity constraints. The implementation of a series of financial reforms in the mid-1980s made it possible to reduce such restrictions. The result, between 1986 and 1997, recalled as the golden period of the Chilean

Since consumption
depends on
expectations about
future income,
when there is greater
uncertainty about
the future, people tend
to save more.

economy, was that national consumption grew at an annual average rate of 8 percent, which was driven by the high growth of household income, good expectations regarding the future, and the expansion of consumer credit. In 1997 the average Chilean enjoyed a consumption level that was more than double the level of 1986.

However, the recession in late 1998 and much of 1999 led to an abrupt drop in consumption. Many people saw their disposable income fall, others lost their jobs, and in general, expectations deteriorated. Even those who managed to keep their jobs had less favorable expectations than before. In a country where the unemployment rate affected about one in ten individuals, most people felt that their jobs were more precarious, so they reduced consumption. In addition, high delinquency rates on consumer credit led financial institutions to impose greater restrictions on their granting of loans.

Although production grew at an average rate of 3.3 percent between 2000 and 2002, during this period consumption increased only 3 percent annually. In addition to the difficulty of accessing financial markets, the persistence of high unemployment rates motivated Chileans to become more cautious about the future and to moderate their consumption. The lowered consumption occurred despite the constant interest rate reductions by the central bank, which sought to strengthen consumption and investment. This shows the powerful effect of consumer expectations: when they deteriorate, they cancel out the effects of traditional macroeconomic policies.

By contrast, beginning in 2003 a period of international prosperity got under way that led to an important improvement in expectations. Private consumption between 2003 and 2008 rose at 6.2 percent annually, while GDP rose at only 4.7 percent annually. Of course, expectations deteriorated with the onset of the recession in late 2008, but this underscores the contrasts between one period and another.

National Saving

The prior analysis was constructed mainly around a representative family. However, we must also understand how to add such individual decisions to obtain national consumption and its complement, *national saving*.

Aggregate saving depends on the age distribution of the population and on income growth, as both characteristics help to determine the wealth of young savers compared to the wealth of old de-savers. The higher the proportion of working-age individuals to the old or the very young, the higher the saving rate of a country. Also, the faster the economy grows, the greater the saving rate.

The effect of the interest rate on saving and consumption is ambiguous in theoretical terms, and the empirical

results are also inconclusive. A higher interest rate results in an incentive to increase saving (because a greater
amount of money in a person's savings account will pay
more interest), which, given the level of income, is known
as a *substitution effect*. This concept alludes to the scenario
in which, when the price of one of two similar goods falls
and everything else remains constant, consumers replace
(or substitute) the amount of the second good consumed
or purchased by consuming a greater amount of the first.
In this case, the interest rate is the price of consumption:
since money can be either spent or saved, when it is not
saved, interest is not being earned. Moreover, the greater
the interest rate, the more individuals tend to decrease
the proportion of their income designated for consumption and increase their saving. However, if the family is a
net creditor (has more financial assets than liabilities), the
increase in the interest rate also increases future income;
therefore, consumption tends to increase and saving is
reduced (the *income effect*). This second concept alludes
to the scenario in which, when relative prices change, the
income of an individual who consumes the goods whose
prices have changed is affected (the individual becomes
relatively richer or poorer than before the price change).
In this case, someone who has more financial assets than
liabilities—say, someone who lends to her neighbors and
is owed to more than she owes others—collects more
money in interest when the interest rates are higher, and

therefore her future income increases when interest rates increase, making her feel richer. Consequently, an increase in interest rates in this situation incentivizes an increase in consumption expenditure (and a decrease in saving).

In the case of a family that is a net debtor (with more liabilities than assets), both effects of the interest rate increase go in the same direction, pushing toward an increase in saving. In general, the substitution effect is considered stronger than the income effect, so that saving tends to respond positively (increase) to interest rate increases.

Alternatively, a lower interest rate decreases saving and increases consumption in net debtors. In the case of net creditors, a lower interest rate increases consumption and decreases saving on the one side (substitution effect) and decreases consumption and increases saving on the other (income effect).

Saving rates differ significantly across countries, reflecting differences in private and government decisions. However, on average, around four-fifths of a country's saving is accounted for by private agents, while the other one-fifth is accounted for by the public sector. Thus, in general, private decisions have a considerably larger weight on a country's overall saving rate.

The United States saves a relatively small portion, less than 17 percent, of its GDP, as shown in the international comparison in table 5. This country is among the developed nations with the lowest saving rates. Southeast Asian economies such as South Korea have saving rates that exceed 35 percent of GDP, while Singapore and China save around 50 percent of GDP. The world average saving rates (as a percentage of GDP) is 24.6 percent, whereas Latin American economies save an average of 18 percent of their output. It should be noted, however, that the fall in international commodity prices in recent years has led many economies to sharply reduce their saving rates; that has been the case with the oil-exporting countries and several Latin American nations.

Table 5 Gross domestic savings in different countries as a percentage of GDP, 2016

China	46.5	Germany	27.2
Singapore	51.2	Uruguay	19.9
Saudi Arabia	31.5	Mexico	21.5
Hong Kong	23.9	Italy	20.4
South Korea	36.0	France	21.1
Peru	21.8	Paraguay	20.2
Argentina	15.7	Brazil	15.8
Chile	22.4	Bolivia	13.3
Japan	24.5	United States	16.9

World Average: 24.6

Source: World Bank, *World Development Indicators.*

Economies that grow faster tend to show higher saving rates than those with lower growth rates. A correlation like this certainly does not demonstrate a causal relationship. It is difficult to know whether high savings determine high growth or whether high growth generates greater saving. In reality, the causality probably goes in both directions.

Why Do They Save So Much in Japan?

To illustrate the difficulties in understanding the determinants of saving and consumption, it may be useful to compare saving activity in Japan with that in the United States. Many analysts have tried to explain the persistent gap since the postwar period between Japan's high saving rates and those of the United States. In 2008, at the onset of the subprime crisis, Japan's domestic saving amounted to 25 percent of GDP, while in the United States it was barely 15.8 percent. Although this gap has diminished in the postcrisis years, Japan's saving in 2016 was 24.5 percent of GDP, still 45 percent higher than in the United States, where it reached 16.9 percent of GDP.

Part of the difference in saving rates is explained by the different way of measuring it in both countries, which may artificially increase the Japanese saving rate and reduce the US rate. Conventionally, expenditure on durable goods such as cars, televisions, and refrigerators is considered consumption. And since families in the United States spend a greater proportion of their income on these durable goods than families in Japan, the US national saving rate turns out to be lower than Japan's. Consequently, the gap between Japanese and US saving rates could decline with an appropriate and standardized definition of consumption. But even after adjusting the definition and data, the differences observed in saving rates between similar age groups in the two countries are still large.

Fumio Hayashi, a prominent analyst of the subject, has argued that Japan's high postwar saving rates may be due to the fact that World War II destroyed the stock of capital in the country, making the return of saving very attractive. It is also possible that high housing prices, in addition to liquidity constraints, force young Japanese workers to save a lot early in their working lives, thereby contributing to raising the saving rate.

In the 1980s, part of the saving rate gap was explained by the fact that, because of Japan's rapid economic growth, young savers were much richer than old de-savers, thereby ensuring a high national saving rate in the country. But such an explanation lost steam when the Japanese economy stagnated in the 1990s.

Other scholars have emphasized that the Japanese tax system promotes more saving than the US system does, while the Japanese social security system provides less coverage, which creates an additional incentive for people to save.

In the final analysis, however, the relative importance of the different factors proposed to explain the difference between saving rates in Japan and the United States continues to be debated. The debate indicates that other factors, such as differences in people's preferences; cultural differences; differences in life expectancy, fertility rates, and aging; and differences in the growth rates of total factor productivity (the fraction of economic growth attributable to technological progress, which we discuss later in the book), should also be considered when analyzing the difference in national saving rates.

PRODUCTIVE INVESTMENT

This chapter analyzes the main characteristics of *investment* (which can be thought of as the accumulation of capital) and the factors that determine it. Investment decisions deserve to be studied for several important reasons. First, adding the study of investment to the analysis of consumption proposed in the previous chapter will allow us to better understand how production is distributed in each period between its current use (consumption) and its future use (investment to increase future consumption). Second, fluctuations in firms' investment play a central role in determining the level of output and employment in the short run; thus, investment has a crucial role in the business cycle. Finally, as discussed in chapter 3, investment contributes significantly to long-term economic growth. In figure 5, it can be clearly seen that, on average, the countries that invest more, grow faster.

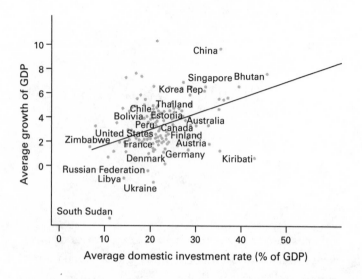

Figure 5 Correlation between growth and investment in selected countries, 1980–2016. *Source:* World Bank, *World Development Indicators.*

The Nature of Investment

Chapter 2 noted that the production of goods and services requires labor, capital, and technology as inputs. When we refer to "capital," we mean a wide range of durable production factors. The same concept encompasses business capital, such as machinery and buildings; environmental capital, such as clean water and fertile soil; and human capital, such as education and work experience. In other words, investment is the part of output that is used to maintain or increase the *stock of capital* in the economy. By increasing the stock of capital, investment spending increases the future productive capacity of the economy.

Just as there are many forms of capital, there are also various forms of investment. *Investment in fixed assets* denotes what companies spend on the plant (the physical structure that occupies a factory or a commercial office) and equipment (machinery and vehicles). *Investment in residential structures* denotes what is spent both on the maintenance of existing housing and on producing new housing. Note, however, that when someone acquires an existing home from someone else, there is no investment, since, from the perspective of the economy, this transaction merely moves capital from one owner to another but does not change the stock of capital. *Inventory investment* denotes the change in the supply of raw materials, semifinished products, and finished goods that have not yet been sold and delivered to the final purchaser over a certain period. An increase in inventories is an investment, while a reduction in inventories is a disinvestment. Another sort of investment is *financial investment*, which denotes the amount of money put into stocks, bonds, options, or investment funds.

Although all sorts of investment are necessary to understand the accumulation of capital within the dynamics of economics, residential investment has played a central role in recent times, as real estate in the United States began to contract in 2006, eventually leading to the outbreak of the subprime crisis and subsequently to a recession in that country and eventually the rest of the world. This type of investment fell 2.2 percent in 2006, 17.8 percent in 2007, and an impressive 25.1 percent and 24 percent in 2008 and 2009, respectively. The evolution of residential investment has been positive after the crisis, reaching levels as high as those seen before the bursting of the real estate bubble (14 percent and 17 percent in 2012 and 2013 respectively) and more moderate levels of growth, around 7 percent, by 2017.

Different Forms of Investment

While fixed investment, stockpiling, and housing are the main categories of investment commonly measured, they are not the only types of investment. There are other ways of spending on durable goods, ways that increase the future productive capacity of the economy. Durable consumer goods such as cars, refrigerators, and washing machines represent consumer services that will last for many periods. Many purchases of new durable consumer goods should then be considered a form of investment. However, since *consumption* is usually defined as including consumer goods such as cars, refrigerators, and washing machines, such purchases are recorded in national accounts as consumption expenses for the period and not as investments. Economists tend to agree on this definition since these items (durable consumer goods) are usually purchased for domestic use and hence are not technically purchased to increase productivity or future production capacity.

The types of capital that have been mentioned so far are called "reproducible" capital because their stock can be increased with increased production. Other kinds of capital, such as land and mining deposits, are "nonreproducible" capital since it is not possible to increase them by producing more. Not only are mining deposits not reproducible, they are also "exhaustible"; that is, the more they are used, the faster they will run out. A broader measure of capital would also include the quality of the environment: air, water, and soil. The deterioration of natural resources should then be counted as a negative investment since it reduces the future productive capacity of the economy. However, little progress has been made in measuring environmental capital.

Official data also overlook many other kinds of intangible capital that should be considered in the stock of national capital. A well-trained labor force is a kind of "human capital," since trained workers increase the productive capacity of the labor force. However, as with durable goods, expenditure on education and training is generally classified—erroneously—as consumption and not as

The deterioration of natural resources should then be counted as a negative investment since it reduces the future productive capacity of the economy.

investment. A similar issue often occurs with research and development expenditures.

When it comes to measuring investment, it is crucial to distinguish between gross and net investment. Gross investment is the total expenditure on capital goods, while net investment is equal to the change in the capital stock from one year to the next. The difference between these two is equal to the depreciation of the capital stock, that is, the amount by which the existing capital is used up or worn out during a given year.

Investment Patterns

Investment is much more volatile than consumption expenditure. This result is not surprising at all. Consumers in general wish to "smooth" their consumption path over time. In other words, they want to have a stable consumption pattern. However, as we will see in this chapter, there are far fewer powerful reasons for an investor (be it a country, a company, or a person) to want a smooth investment trajectory, and indeed there may be compelling reasons for investment to spike and slow at various times.

If we compare fixed capital formation among industrialized countries, measured as a percentage of GDP, we notice that in the United States this coefficient is among the lowest. Japan has consistently invested about one-third of its GDP in the past decades, although in recent years that share has declined considerably. Fixed capital formation in France was between 20 percent and 25 percent of GDP for most of the same period. This coefficient fluctuated between 15 percent and 20 percent in the United States and the United Kingdom, which are among the lowest in the industrialized world.

In Latin America, the picture is mixed: while some countries invest a considerable portion of their GDP, others invest less than developed nations. However, the gap is even larger when compared to Southeast Asian countries, which usually allocate more than a quarter of their output to capital formation and in the case of China it is over 40 percent of GDP.

From this perspective, it is not surprising that over the past forty years the per capita income growth of the Asian tigers was three times greater than that of Latin America. There are other differences between these nations that explain such a divergence, such as the quality of institutions, adherence to the rule of law, and an outward orientation. However, almost half of the gap is attributable to differences in capital accumulation between the two regions; hence, governments are interested in promoting both internal and external investment, to grow more.

Determinants of Investment

An interesting empirical regularity is that—in the short term—investment responds to the growth rate of a country or region. When growth accelerates, investment increases, and when growth slows down, investment decreases. This relationship is explained by the fact that companies invest to expand future productive capacity and therefore need to be able to somehow predict the future state of the economy. One of the main signs of this future state is precisely the current growth of production. High rates of GDP growth are generally interpreted as a sign of future prosperity.

Another factor that is central to investment decisions is the comparison between the *cost of capital*, which is closely related to the interest rate, and the profitability of a given project. When the interest rate falls, the cost of financing investment is lower, encouraging greater investment. It is precisely through this relationship that governments try to influence investment decisions. For example, an increase in the corporate income tax would reduce the net (private) profit of the investment, while an increase in the corporate tax credit (e.g., through a policy of *accelerated depreciation*) would increase the private return of an investment.

Not all individuals or companies can freely borrow at the market interest rate to finance their investments, even when a project is profitable. When a company is credit rationed, investment depends not only on the interest rate and the profitability of the project but also on the cash flow of the company. This phenomenon, which is called *credit rationing*, appears mainly in two cases: when the government establishes a "ceiling" to the interest rate, putting it below market equilibrium, and when credit institutions fail to accurately assess the risks of lending money to certain debtors. The problem of credit rationing is especially experienced by small and medium-sized enterprises (SMEs) and people who do not have assets that serve as collateral for a loan.

One should also consider that many investments are irreversible to some degree. This means that if things do not turn out as expected, the investment can be undone only by incurring very high costs, or not at all. For example, it is not easy to transform a car manufacturing plant into a textile plant. The potential *irreversibility of investment* can lead to the postponing of projects in an environment of high uncertainty as people wait for a more favorable environment. Achieving greater macroeconomic stability is therefore key for a country that wants to achieve higher levels of investment.

To conclude this chapter, the following discussion of *Keynesian animal spirits* illustrates how John Maynard Keynes, one of the early leaders of macroeconomic analysis, understood investment more than seventy years ago.

Keynesian Animal Spirits

John Maynard Keynes is undoubtedly the most influential advocate of the perception that many of the fluctuations in investment reflect increases or reductions in optimism, not explained by changes in the fundamental variables of the economy. In his 1936 book, *The General Theory of Employment, Interest and Money*, Keynes attributes investment decisions to instinct (animal spirits, in his term) rather than precise mathematical calculations:

> Most, probably, of our decisions to do something positive, the full consequences of which will be drawn out over many days to come, can only be taken as the result of animal spirits—a spontaneous urge to action rather than inaction, and not as the outcome of a weighted average of quantitative benefits multiplied by quantitative probabilities. (Keynes, 161–162)

Keynes thought that economic fluctuations are caused to a large extent by ups and downs of investment, which are both the result of waves of optimism or pessimism that provoke the instinct.

One of the most important issues in macroeconomics is to understand the causes of economic fluctuations, which are also known as economic or business cycles.

Some recent research attempts to formalize Keynes's intuitive perception of the importance of investor confidence and animal spirits (instinct) in determining economic and investment fluctuations. The argument is that the investment decisions of a company are determined by expectations regarding future economic activity. When business owners feel optimistic and expect the economy to grow, they invest and produce more, and later expect a high demand for their products. At the same time, this motivates suppliers to invest and produce more, and so on, thereby fueling an economic boom. Conversely, if investors are pessimistic about the economic future, they reduce investment, lay off their employees, and produce less, perhaps triggering a recession.

In the United States, private investment began to decline in 2005 and was already well below earlier levels by mid-2007, before the onset of the subprime crisis. These facts are explained by the growing distrust of housing prices in the real estate market in the face of rumors about the existence of a bubble that could explode, which generated pessimism among investors. As well, private consumption was less volatile than investment, although it also began to adjust before the subprime crisis began.

What happened during the last financial crisis gave rise to a debate about the arguments used by John Maynard Keynes almost eighty years ago. To what extent can a crisis of this magnitude be explained by fundamental factors of the economy? And further, to what extent are crises driven by animal spirits? This is a discussion that remains latent in the economics discipline. Alan Greenspan, president of the Federal Reserve for much of the time leading up to the subprime crisis (1987–2006), was criticized for not recognizing in time that a financial bubble was brewing and that stricter regulation could have been necessary. At the end of the day, the high price of housing and the proliferation of complex financial derivatives had elements of animal spirits that were not foreseen.

In the same way that investor expectations sustained excessively high prices in the financial market for years, the subsequent pessimism of seeing the bubble explode was one of the triggers of the 2009 financial crisis. In other words, investors' expectations can become *self-fulfilling prophecies*; that is, when everyone thinks there will be a recession, nobody invests, and the recession in fact arrives. When everyone thinks the economy will grow, everyone invests and produces more since growth is expected to become a reality.

This conclusion may be frustrating for a central bank. If the economic cycle depends on mood swings, how could one possibly maintain sustained growth? According to Keynes, governments should aim to maintain "a political and social atmosphere which is congenial to the average business man." The steps toward achieving this goal include maintaining sound fiscal and monetary policies,

Investors' expectations can become self-fulfilling prophecies; that is, when everyone thinks there will be a recession, nobody invests, and the recession in fact arrives.

ensuring respect for the rule of law and basic property rights, and avoiding social instability.

Foreign Direct Investment

Foreign direct investment (FDI) is the total investment made by foreign investors in national enterprises. FDI occurs when an investor establishes foreign business operations or acquires foreign business assets, in this way establishing ownership or a controlling interest in a foreign company. In that sense, the concept of FDI cannot be directly assimilated to the concept of fixed capital formation, but there is a strong positive correlation between the two.

In some countries, FDI represents a large share of overall investment, making significant contributions to economic growth. Nonetheless, the contribution of FDI to the local economy is generally much more than an increase in overall investment. When a developing country receives FDI, the foreign investors likely bring new technologies that were not yet available to the local economy, increasing productivity growth. Along these lines, FDI can also be associated with new training programs for workers and fostering human capital accumulation.

Although FDI tends to have higher returns in emerging markets, the lack of clear property rights, as well as macroeconomic and political instability, can discourage the flow of capital to these economies. In fact, according to the United Nations' *World Investment Report 2018*, FDI inflows are equivalent to 11.9 percent of fixed capital formation in OECD countries, while they are only 7.4 percent in developing economies. Therefore, to spur FDI in emerging markets, improving economic and political institutions is key. Finally, FDI must be carried out in a context of absolute respect for local and international regulations, safeguarding the rights of workers and domestic investors.

THE CURRENT ACCOUNT AND EXTERNAL DEBT

The current account balance—a component of the *balance of payments* that was discussed in chapter 1—is a measure of the exports of goods and services from a country to the rest of the world, minus that country's imports of goods and services from the rest of the world, plus the net transfers that the country receives from abroad. Put simply, it reflects whether a country is spending more or less than what it produces.

Some countries may spend beyond their income for some years. The best example of this is the United States, which in the year leading up to the subprime crisis had a current account deficit equivalent to 5.8 percent of GDP in 2006, or about $806 billion. In the years following the financial crisis, this deficit in the United States fell, and in 2017 the country ran a deficit of around 2.4 percent of GDP ($466 billion). A low national saving rate, an excess of private spending, and fiscal deficits have contributed to generate an imbalance, which is reflected in the United States' current account. Other countries spend less than they produce, such as China, which, thanks to its very high rate of saving, has had a positive current account balance for more than two decades.

If a country has a current account deficit (a negative balance), it will increase its net debt vis-à-vis the rest of the world. Sooner or later, the country must reduce its domestic spending to cover the debt it has accumulated. In this chapter, we analyze what is behind the current account balance and the role played by spending, saving, and investment in forming the main macroeconomic variables of a country.

The Different Interpretations of the Current Account

A country's trade and financial transactions with the rest of the world are measured through its balance of payments, a main component of which is the current account balance. There are four ways to understand and interpret the current account balance. Each of them illustrates different aspects of this important macroeconomic variable.

The first highlights the fact that in an open economy, national savings need not be equal to national investment, as they would have to be in a closed economy. In this sense, the current account measures the difference between saving and investment in a country. When national savings are greater than domestic investment, the country has a current account surplus; when savings are less than investment, the country has a current account deficit.

What happens when a country saves more than it invests? Its residents—families and businesses—accumulate financial assets over the rest of the world. The national economy lends money to foreigners, perhaps by investing in an external bank, buying bonds issued by a foreign company, or providing capital to finance investment projects abroad. Therefore, the current account is also defined as the variation of a country's net financial assets abroad. Put another way, it is the change in the *net external assets position* (NEAP), which is also called the net international investment position (NIIP) of a country. When this position is positive, the country is a *net creditor* to the rest of the world, and when it is negative, the country is a *net debtor*.

In many countries, especially in the developing world, the NEAP is negative, since the current account balance has been in deficit for a long time. In this way, and to finance higher investment rates, an economy complements domestic savings with *external savings* (money lent to other countries). However, the high and persistent levels of debt in developing countries have attracted much attention and incited controversy during the past three decades. In the 1980s, this became known as the third world debt crisis.

Note that the United States' current account deficits began to expand from the 1980s onward, turning the country into the largest net debtor in the world, after being the world's largest international creditor. The external imbalance in the United States was one of the causes of the depreciation of the dollar between 2002 and 2013, a sign of the rest of the world's reluctance to lend to the world's largest economy once it exceeded certain limits. In fact, in 2006, the current account deficit reached a historical level of almost 6 percent of GDP, which, in the eyes of many experts, should be unsustainable. Several analysts advocated reducing the external imbalance, which was due to high energy prices at the time, expansive monetary and fiscal policies, and rising old-age pension costs. With the subprime crisis, in 2008 the country reduced its deficit to 4.6 percent of GDP, and to 2.6 percent in 2009, because of the low availability of external financing and a significant fall in imports caused by the crisis. By 2017 the current account deficit had declined to 2.4 percent of GDP.

Despite its magnitude, however, the United States' problem is not as large as Mexico's or Argentina's, for instance, when one considers income level. The United States' net international liabilities in 2017 represented 40 percent of its GDP, while the net debt of Mexico during the 1980s was much higher than half its GDP, and in 2002 in Argentina, owing to the abrupt depreciation of the currency and the fall in output, this ratio reached 130 percent of the value of GDP.

The current account is also defined as the difference between the total income of an economy, the gross national income, and total expenditure. In this sense, countries face a current account deficit if they spend more than they produce. High current account deficits indicate that the residents of a country spend well above their income. In several emerging economies, the public sector contributes significantly to excess spending. Therefore, an effective way to improve the current account is by reducing the fiscal deficit, which is simply the difference between government savings and investment.

A final definition, which is very much related to the way in which balance of payments accounts are arranged, indicates that the current account balance is equal to the sum of net exports (also known as the trade balance) plus *net payments to domestic production factors* (NFPs, for net factor payments)—corresponding to interest earned on net external assets, net income on the investment of residents abroad, and net remittances sent by nationals working abroad—plus *unilateral transfers*, that is, donations received from other nations. Generally, the NFP balance is negative for developing nations because they accumulate net external debt and are strong recipients of foreign investment.

Some decades ago, according to this last definition of current account, it was considered that to improve the current account, a country had to resort to trade policy—for example, by subsidizing exports and imposing import tariffs. However, that vision has changed, and trade imbalances are now understood from a broader and more comprehensive macroeconomic perspective, which sees a current account deficit as an indicator that a country saves little in relation to what it invests and spends beyond its income.

What Lies behind a Current Account Balance?

To get more familiar with the external accounts, we provide the current account balances of several countries in the table 6. Note that in the United States, the current account deficit is almost completely attributable to a trade deficit, while "other goods, services, and rents" (e.g., the return on direct foreign investment and external assets) mainly offset this deficit. In Japan, the component "other goods, services, and income" is the main cause of the current account surplus, since net payments to factors from abroad are positive, reflecting its position as a net international creditor. For Brazil, a major net debtor, the current account showed a deficit of $10 billion in 2017, despite having a trade surplus of $61 billion. The difference

Table 6 Composition of the current account in selected countries (billions of current US dollars, 2017)

	United States	Japan	Brazil	El Salvador	Mexico	Chile	Spain
Trade balance	−821	39	61	−5	−15	7	−25
Exports	1,529	682	214	5	405	69	314
Imports	2,350	643	153	9	421	61	339
Other goods, services, and rents	469	177	−74	−1	−32	−13	63
Travel	68	16	−13	0	11	1	46
Interests and dividends	−8	110	−39	−1	−22	−10	−22
Other	408	51	−21	0	−20	−5	39
Unilateral transfers	−115	−19	3	5	28	2	−13
Official transfers	−16	−4	0	0	0	2	−7
Workers' remittances	−48	−1	0	5	28	0	0
Other	−50	−14	2	0	0	0	−6
Current account balance	−466	196	−10	−1	−19	−4	26
Gross domestic product	19,391	4,872	2,055	28	1,149	277	1,314

Source: International Monetary Fund, *Macroeconomic and Financial Data: Balance of Payments and International Investment Position Statistics,* 2018.

between these figures can be greatly explained by the huge interest payments on Brazil's external debt.

Among service payments, workers' remittances are a very important source of international reserves in the current account of countries such as Mexico and El Salvador. For this item, in 2017 Mexico received an income of 2.4 percent of its GDP, which surpasses the *trade balance* deficit of 1.3 percent of GDP but is not enough to offset the 2.7 percent of GDP represented by payments for services and rent. Note also that workers' remittances represent a significant outflow of funds from the United States, while the opposite occurs in El Salvador, Brazil, and Mexico, as workers go to the United States, attracted by higher wages, and send money to their families in their home nations.

In other countries, tourism is a very important source of foreign currency. Indeed, tourism is the main export of Spain, for example, with a net contribution of almost $46 billion in 2017, or about 3.5 percent of GDP.

Chile presented a current account deficit in 2017, a situation repeated since 2011, after several years marked by large surpluses, reflecting an external situation characterized by high copper prices (except for the year 2009, when the subprime crisis broke out). This figure was compounded by a positive trade balance, which was more than offset by interest payments on foreign loans and the profits on foreign direct investment.

Determinants of the Current Account

The factors that influence the current account are several, all linked to the variables that determine saving, investment, and the fiscal deficit. For example, an increase in the interest rate tends to improve the current account balance of a small country by increasing saving and reducing investment. On the other hand, an increase in the profitability of investment projects tends to reduce the current account balance since it reduces saving and increases investment.

As we mentioned earlier in this chapter, a reduction in saving or an increase in investment tends to reduce the current account surplus (or increase the current account deficit). Said simply, if national saving is reduced, then either more financing is required from foreign capital or the country will have less domestic investment. Either way, the country's NEAP deteriorates, along with an increase in the current account deficit (or a decrease in the current account surplus). On the other hand, if domestic investment becomes more profitable, it will be financed by more domestic savings, as well as by (foreign) capital inflows. In this sense, the rest of the world will be lending more money to the country, hence increasing its position as a net debtor to the rest of the world, which results in a greater current account deficit (or a lower current account surplus).

Another crucial factor, because of its relation to saving, is the income flow of an economy's residents. In many countries, income may fall temporarily because of weather disasters or other exogenous shocks hitting a major economic sector. Some examples are an Andean country affected by the El Niño phenomenon or a Caribbean country devastated by a hurricane. The main conclusions about the determination of consumption predict that individuals will want to maintain a relatively stable level of consumption when faced with a temporary reduction in income, which decreases aggregate saving and results in a deterioration of the current account.

In countries that are dependent on the export of raw materials, a temporary drop in the price of their main export product (soybeans in Argentina, copper in Chile, oil in Colombia, Ecuador, Nigeria, Saudi Arabia, and Venezuela, or natural gas in Bolivia). would reduce national income, which would result in lower national saving and, therefore, a deterioration in the current account balance.

A permanent decline in national income, however, should have little or no effect on the current account, since total consumption expenditure would have to fall by about the same amount as the reduction in income. Of course, if the permanent shock is misinterpreted as transitory, then the current account will deteriorate anyway. In general, the optimal response to this type of shock is summarized in the phrase "finance a temporary shock and adjust to a permanent shock." Here, "finance" refers to accumulating a current account deficit and "adjust" implies reducing consumption sufficiently to absorb the shock without resorting to external debt. Even before the collapse of Lehman Brothers in September 2008, commodity-dependent countries were experiencing the opposite situation, thanks to the boom in international prices, which allowed them to accumulate large current account surpluses. However, with the recession and the consequent collapse of commodity prices, current account balances deteriorated sharply in the region.

The above analysis assumes that debt can and will be paid. However, some debtors fall into *insolvency* (inability to fully service debts using current and future incomes); while others, who could pay, choose not to, knowing that it is very difficult for external creditors to demand repayment of their loans. The difficulty of enforcing credit commitments is especially great when it comes to *sovereign loans*, that is, those granted to foreign governments. When a potential creditor understands that a debtor may have motivations not to pay or may simply have difficulty paying, the creditor will restrict the supply of credit to that debtor to a level that the creditor thinks can be recovered.

The sovereign debt crisis in Greece illustrates the need to thoroughly evaluate a debtor before delivering credit. With the outbreak of the subprime crisis in the United

States and the ensuing European crisis in 2009, the European Central Bank acted to find a solution and try to stop the spread of damages. Measures were formulated to assist banks in member states, which eventually revealed the specific needs of each country, particularly in the cases of Greece, Ireland, and Portugal, which requested full financial assistance for the tensions they were facing in the sovereign debt market. To rescue some member states, conditions of fiscal discipline were imposed on aid recipients. In the case of Greece, whose *fiscal deficit* and *public debt* revealed at the time of the crisis turned out to be much larger than previously thought, several conditions of fiscal austerity were imposed to restructure its sovereign debt.

The International Monetary Fund

In the global context, one aspect related to the current account in periods of adverse shocks is the maintenance of a secure international payments system, which is monitored by the International Monetary Fund (IMF). The IMF was created immediately after World War II to assist countries that were experiencing difficulty making their external payments and to promote the international stability of the monetary system. The fundamental pattern in IMF lending policies is to financially support nations facing transitory problems and to recommend macroeconomic adjustments in the event of permanent shocks.

In 1963 the IMF created the Compensatory Financing Facility (CFF), a credit fund explicitly designed to lend to countries experiencing temporary declines in their exports. In 1988, the program was slightly modified and transformed into the Compensatory and Contingency Financing Facility (CCFF) to broaden its range of action beyond the event of a fall in exports. The IMF provides many other types of loans, including those to support structural adjustment programs in the poorest countries, help in stabilization programs, and assist in the management of certain external debt crises.

To qualify for a CCFF loan, the country must demonstrate in detail that it has suffered a reduction in its export earnings and that the decrease is transient. If the fall seems to be permanent, the IMF does not provide a loan through the CCFF; instead, it advises the country to restructure and reduce its spending to absorb the fall in its exports. The idea of financing a temporary shock but recommending that a country adjust to a permanent shock represents both a *normative* (what must happen) and *positive* (what will happen) view of the current account. However, the positive approach tends to fall short in predicting what happens to the current account.

The positive view of the current account depends on several assumptions: that people act in a rational way and take the future into account, that they know how to distinguish temporary from permanent shocks, and that they can raise money freely in response to such shocks. However, such assumptions are often unrealistic. When governments borrow or lend, they do not regularly incorporate long-term information into their decisions.

For example, when several developing countries improved their *terms of trade* (the relative price of exports to imports) in the late 1970s, they did not accumulate a surplus in their current account, as predicted by the theory. On the contrary, their respective governments often acted as if the terms of trade had improved on a permanent basis, and spent the total gain on their real income, although it was likely that such a gain would not last long. Mexico, for example, spent almost all the money it received for oil exports when prices soared in 1979–1980. When the terms of trade turned around in the early 1980s, Mexico and other governments in the same situation encountered unsustainable levels of spending and enormous political difficulties in cutting spending and bringing it back to manageable levels. In many cases, a deep economic and political crisis was necessary for government spending to fall back to sustainable levels.

When Azerbaijan and Pakistan suffered a fall in export earnings as a result of a poor cotton harvest attributable to climatic problems in late 1998, each received an IMF loan through the CCFF. The IMF authorities noted, however, that the reason for lending to them was that the deficit was triggered by poor weather rather than by a drop in world cotton prices. If the fall in cotton prices had been the culprit, it would have been much more difficult to prove that the decline in export earnings was a transitory fluctuation.

The global economic crisis of 2008–2009 sharpened the need to watch the flow of capital between countries— among other variables that also determine the sustainability of an imbalance—with greater care. In 2008 the IMF responded to the global financial crisis by mobilizing resources to improve support to its member countries: it offered loans and policy solutions and introduced reforms to its own operations to better attend to the needs of each country. The IMF increased its lending capacity through increases in membership fees—reflected in the 14th General Review of Quotas, approved in 2010—and by securing large indebtedness agreements, reflected in the creation of New Loan Agreements (NLAs), which were added to the existing loan agreements.

In addition, the IMF reformed the framework for loan delivery, placing greater emphasis on crisis prevention. For this purpose, lines of credit were created with amounts and conditions better adjusted to the needs of the countries, such as the Flexible Credit Line (FCL), introduced in 2009 for countries such as Colombia, Mexico, and Poland, and the Precautionary Liquidity Line (PLL), which

The global economic crisis sharpened the need to watch the flow of capital between countries with greater care.

was created for and used by Macedonia and Morocco. The PLL was designed to give member countries the chance to flexibly meet their liquidity needs; candidates for receiving a PPL had to have solid economic fundamentals, a solid institutional framework, and a commitment to maintaining sound policies in the future, but with some limited remaining vulnerabilities that excluded them from using the FCL. The IMF also strengthened its surveillance system to operate in a more globalized and interconnected economy, and in 2014 it published its *Triennial Surveillance Review*, proposing greater and better multilateral macro-financial surveillance as one of the operational priorities. This report highlights the relevance of monitoring global imbalances and their sustainable financing, among other priorities, to ensure greater global stability.

FISCAL POLICY AND ITS
IMPLICATIONS

For some historians, fiscal excesses were a key cause of the decline of the Roman Empire. Others conclude that fiscal problems also played a decisive role in the decline of Spain after the reign of Charles V. Also, the tribulations of Brazil in 1998, 2001–2002, and 2015–2017 and the crisis in Greece since 2009 have had a strong fiscal component. These historical cases over the last two thousand years suggest that one must be especially careful with the fiscal accounts.

Government spending, saving, and investment have important effects on the main macroeconomic variables: national (private, nongovernment) savings and investment naturally imply an effect on the current account balance, among other variables.

Moreover, public saving and investment are part of the general fiscal policy of the government, which shapes the pattern of spending decisions, taxation, and the indebtedness of the public sector. In this chapter we analyze fiscal policy and its macroeconomic effects.

Government Revenues and Expenditures

One of the main instruments of public finances is the *fiscal or government budget*, which describes public sector revenues and expenditures. The difference between the two is known as the *fiscal balance*: if it is positive, there is a surplus; if it is negative, there is a deficit. The fiscal balance determines the amount of credit that the public sector can grant or must acquire. Moreover, the fiscal deficit is equal to the increase in government debt, when it cannot be financed by monetary issuance or the sale of assets.

Taxes, usually the most important source of public revenue, fall into three broad categories: *income and property taxes* paid by individuals and businesses, and *expenditure taxes*, which are associated with the purchase of goods. The first two are also known as *direct taxes*; the latter corresponds to *indirect taxes*. Governments of developed economies usually obtain a large part of their revenue from direct taxes.

In the United States, for example, the main source of fiscal revenue comes from direct taxes, which account for more than 80 percent of the government's total income and are mainly paid by individuals. Revenue from direct taxes comes from taxes on personal and corporate income and capital gains, taxes on payroll and labor, and taxes on property. Developing country governments, on the other hand, tend to receive most of their revenue through indirect taxes, which include levies on goods and services and on international trade. One reason why indirect taxes are so important as a source of public income in developing countries is that they are easier to collect than *income taxes*. However, a tax system based on indirect taxes tends to be regressive, since the taxes paid by the poor represent a greater portion of their income than those paid by better-off individuals. On the other hand, a tax system concentrated more heavily on direct taxes may be progressive. This is because direct taxes are charged as a fraction of people's income and property value, and therefore may be implemented differently according to people's income level. This way, higher tax rates may be charged to people of higher income and lower tax rates to people of lower income.

The profits of companies and state agencies are another source of government revenues, although generally less significant. In many natural resource–rich developing countries, the revenues of state-owned companies usually contribute a substantial proportion of public revenues, as in Colombia, Nigeria, Saudi Arabia, or Venezuela with oil, or to a lesser extent in Chile and Peru with copper.

A tax system based on indirect taxes tends to be regressive, since the taxes paid by the poor represent a greater portion of their income than those paid by better-off individuals.

However, countries that have abundant natural resource revenues tend to expand their fiscal spending excessively when commodity prices rise (as occurred during the first decade of the 2000s), resulting in unsustainable fiscal deficits when the prices of these resources go down.

Public spending can be grouped into four categories: (1) *government consumption*, which includes the salaries that the government pays to public employees, as well as purchases of goods and services for current consumption; (2) *government investment*, which encompasses a variety of forms of capital expenditure, such as the construction of roads and ports; (3) *transfers to the private sector*, which include retirement pensions, unemployment insurance, veterans' benefits, and other benefits; and (4) *interest paid on public debt*.

Fiscal spending can be divided into two major groups: *current expenditures*, which include the payment of wages, the purchase of goods and services, the payment of interest and transfers, and government investment.

Table 7 presents the structure of government expenditures in developed and developing countries. Note that a huge portion goes to current expenditure items, while investment accounts for a very low portion of total expenditure (see "Capital Expenditures" in table 7), usually less than 10 percent. However, it is possible that more than one investment category is perhaps classified erroneously as consumption, as in the example seen in chapter 7:

expenditure on durable goods is almost always classified as consumption, and therefore what is classified as capital expenditure is generally underestimated.

Strikingly, two of the developed countries in table 7—Germany and the United Kingdom—devote less than 5 percent of government spending to investment, even though the share of capital expenditure increased significantly in Germany immediately after its reunification. Note also that developing countries, such as Brazil, allocate a high proportion of their budget to servicing external and internal debt, although this is also an important component of public spending in the United States.

Before continuing the analysis, it is necessary to add a warning about the economic meaning of the terms *government* and *public sector*. The first term can have very different meanings, depending on the context. The *central government* refers to governmental and administrative agencies at the national level. The *general government* includes central government and local and regional governments, as well as decentralized institutions (e.g., national pension funds and state universities). Together, the general government and nonfinancial public enterprises are called the *nonfinancial public sector*. Finally, the *consolidated public sector* adds the nonfinancial public sector to the accounts of the central bank and financial institutions owned by the state.

Table 7 Structure of central government expenditures in selected countries (% total expenditures)

Country	Year	Current Expenditure (%)				Other expenditures (%)	Capital expenditures (%)
		Salaries	Goods and services	Interest payments	Subsidies and transfers		
Germany	2016	16.6	10.4	3.1	59.7	5.5	4.8
Chile	2016	27.6	12.7	3.2	35.2	17.3	4.1
Hong Kong	2015	21.5	33.7	0.5	15.4	25.9	2.9
United States	2016	25.7	14.4	10.1	42.8	0.1	6.9
Hungary	2016	22.9	14.7	6.7	37.8	10.4	7.6
United Kingdom	2016	22.5	20.0	6.1	43.3	4.4	3.7
Thailand	2016	34.5	32.5	4.5	18.2	5.7	4.6
Brazil	2016	26.5	11.0	21.2	35.2	2.9	3.1

Source: International Monetary Fund, *Macroeconomic and Financial Data: Government Finance Statistics*, 2018.

Savings, Investment and the Fiscal Deficit

It is important to integrate the government sector into the analysis of the current account of the balance of payments. In the previous chapter, the current account was defined as saving minus investment. Therefore, it can also be stated that it is equal to the private financial surplus (private saving minus private investment) plus the surplus of the public sector (public saving minus public investment). The public surplus is also known as the budget surplus or fiscal surplus. Consequently, keeping the private surplus fixed, a fall in the fiscal surplus—or an increase in the deficit—would lead to a deterioration of the current account. So, one way to reduce the current account deficit to sustainable levels is by cutting the fiscal deficit.

An example of the importance of the fiscal deficit was its role in the process of monetary unification that occurred in the EU. In December 1991, European countries agreed to reduce their deficits as a condition for participating in a common currency, the euro, as stipulated in the Maastricht Treaty.

From the Maastricht Treaty to the Euro Crisis

In 1957, the *Treaty of Rome* began the process of European economic unification. This process began as a free trade agreement between six nations and culminated in 1999 with the launch of the *Economic and Monetary Union* (EMU) of the EU.

The member countries of the EMU are a subgroup of EU members that use the same currency, the euro, and whose monetary policies are decided by the European Central Bank (ECB). A cornerstone of monetary unification was the *Treaty of Maastricht*, signed by the members of the EU in December 1991. One of the main objectives of the agreement was to achieve a certain convergence in the economic policies of the countries that make up the EU, to facilitate the establishment of a common monetary policy. With this, several convergence criteria were established as requirements for admission to the single currency. These criteria were essentially four: inflation control, a cap on public debt and fiscal deficits, exchange rate stability, and a cap on long-term interest rates.

In the area of fiscal policy, the criterion was that the government deficit, planned or effective, should never exceed 3 percent of GDP; in addition, the government could not hold debt exceeding 60 percent of GDP (the difference between government deficit and government debt is that the former is only the negative difference between government income and government spending, while the latter is the result of the government borrowing money to cover budget deficits or to finance programs and includes securities, bonds, and bills issued by the government). Many consider that the Maastricht Treaty was the main influence for the improvement of fiscal indicators in Europe during the 1990s and that it played a very important role in stopping the increasing share of GDP represented by government spending.

Furthermore, to adopt the euro, a country could not have an inflation rate exceeding an inflation reference value established for the entire euro zone; the country had to participate in the exchange rate mechanism (ERM) under the European Economic and Monetary System for at least two consecutive years; and long-term interest rates (average yields for ten-year government bonds in the past year) had to be no more than two percentage points higher than an established reference value.

Despite this initial impulse, the fiscal situation deteriorated toward the end of the 2000s, as several European countries exhibited levels of public debt and fiscal deficits well above the limits established in the Maastricht Treaty. By 2009, Greece's public debt had reached about 127 percent of GDP and its fiscal deficit had reached 15 percent of GDP, which was twice the agreed-on limit for debt and five times the limit for the deficit. Portugal, another of the countries most affected by the crisis, also exhibited a deteriorating fiscal situation, with a public debt of 84 percent of GDP and a fiscal deficit of almost 10 percent. Beyond these cases, toward the end of the 2000s most of the countries in the euro zone were not complying with the fiscal requirements to which they had committed.

Failure to comply with fiscal discipline led to a deep crisis in the euro zone as of 2009. The situation was particularly critical for Greece, Portugal, and Ireland, and the EU decided to adopt rescue plans to assist their economies. In the case of Greece, the first rescue came in 2010 in the form of €110 billion as a loan to prevent the country from defaulting on its debts, with the requirement that the country had to implement strict cuts in expenditures and tax increases. In 2011, Portugal and Ireland needed rescues of €78 billion and €85 billion, respectively; however, in Ireland it was more a case of a collapse of its banking system resulting from the crisis rather than a case of fiscal profligacy.

After the effects of the euro-zone crisis, in 2012 the Treaty on Stability, Coordination and Governance in the Economic and Monetary Union, also referred to as the European Fiscal Compact, was signed, which set new "rules of the game" for the group. These fiscal rules established that the annual structural deficit (or the government deficit calculated with medium-term estimates of key economic variables and long-term estimates of economic activity, excluding cyclical fluctuations); sanctions were also set for countries whose fiscal deficit exceeded 3 percent of GDP, and the agreement established the obligation to reduce public debt to no more than 60 percent of GDP in a maximum term of twenty years. Even though public debt levels have remained high, the magnitude of the fiscal deficits has decreased considerably in the years following this pact. Undoubtedly, achieving convergence of the public debt toward the established levels will not be easy, but everything indicates that the countries of the euro zone are handling their fiscal policy with greater rigor.

The Cyclical Pattern of the Fiscal Deficit

The economic cycle also plays an important role in determining the size of the fiscal deficit. Deficits tend to rise in recessions, while the fiscal balance tends to improve during booms. Two factors contribute to this pattern. First, tax collection tends to increase dramatically during booms and fall during recessions. Because tax collection increases and falls in line with the business cycle, it is said to be *procyclical*. Second, certain categories of government spending, such as transfers to the unemployed, are *countercyclical*, meaning that spending in these categories tends to increase in recessive periods and decrease when the economy recovers. The cyclical nature of the fiscal deficit means it is not easy to determine whether the government spends more than it receives because of internal reasons or because of problems associated with the economic cycle. To solve this problem, several countries calculate an indicator known as the *structural fiscal balance*, which is the fiscal balance that would exist if the economy were at its *potential level of output*, that is, excluding the influence of booms and recessions. This is a hypothetical fiscal balance; it is not actualized, and it is calculated chiefly to have a benchmark or target for the government's performance. A way of achieving this target is by creating a *structural balance rule*, which legislates that the government must fix fiscal expenditures in a way that guarantees a certain structural deficit (or surplus) as a specific percentage of GDP during the year or period. This rule has the advantage of providing an automatic stabilization mechanism: a moderate fiscal deficit is allowed in recessions, while during booms the government commits to a surplus.

A structural balance rule can be even more beneficial in the case of countries that are rich in natural resources, whose revenues grow with positive price shocks. A sudden abundance of resources can induce a false sense of security in an economy and could encourage politicians to borrow and expand public spending excessively, which is unsustainable when the income from natural resources drops significantly. A good example of this is the Netherlands, which, with the discovery of natural gas, coupled with global shocks in oil prices during the 1970s and 1980s, expanded public employment and consumption to levels that later proved difficult to reverse.

Though fiscal rules have been, in general, a useful tool to control fiscal spending, there are still many aspects of fiscal policy that remain at the discretion of the fiscal authority. As a complement to the fiscal rule, some countries have implemented a fiscal council consisting of a board of experts tasked with supervising fiscal policy. While the institution of a fiscal council is popular among developed countries (the United States, Germany, Denmark, and most OECD members have one), its implementation is less common in developing economies. For example, in South America only Chile, Peru, Colombia, and Paraguay have implemented a fiscal council, but such councils are not always completely independent of the central government.

The Complementary Roles of Fiscal and Monetary Policy

The last global crisis of 2008–2009 and its aftermath show how fiscal and monetary policy can play complementary roles in the economy. When the crisis started, several governments began implementing short-term fiscal plans to foster economic activity and avoid deeper economic and social effects. At the same time, central banks began to implement sharp decreases in their monetary policy rates in order to accommodate the economy to the more adverse internal and external conditions. Most economists agree that this coordinated response was key to preventing a deeper fall of the global economy and to a faster recovery compared to the fall and recovery associated with the Great Depression of 1929.

On average, the G-20 economies (a selected group of countries that represent almost 85 percent of global GDP) implemented fiscal plans that involved spending approximately 2 percent of their GDP from 2008 to 2010. However, according to IMF estimates, the United States' fiscal stimulus was considerably larger, with a public expenditure of around 4.9 percent of GDP on discretionary fiscal measures in a three-year period. Others with large fiscal plans were China, spending 4.4 percent of GDP, and Germany, with 3.5 percent of GDP, while Japan implemented a fiscal plan of 2.2 percent of GDP.

These fiscal plans comprised a variety of measures, such as increasing the fiscal spending on infrastructure (especially transportation networks), providing transfers to the most vulnerable sectors of the population, strengthening unemployment benefits, or supporting small and medium-sized enterprises (SMEs) with soft credits. In some cases, fiscal plans also included temporary cuts in personal income taxes or indirect taxes.

On the monetary policy side, the economic stimulus was also large. For instance, the effective Fed funds rate (the monetary policy rate of the United States) was reduced from 5.25 percent in 2007 to 0 percent during 2009 and remained at this zero level for several years. The

Federal Reserve also implemented an unconventional monetary policy called quantitative easing (QE), which, as discussed in chapter 4, consisted in the purchase of long-term financial assets to expand the monetary supply.

The quick reaction to the (subprime) crisis, complemented by a sizable fiscal plan with a highly expansive monetary policy, gave significantly different results from those seen after the more hesitant reactions to the Great Depression of 1929. The difference in responses to these two global scenarios most likely contributed to the unemployment rate increasing to only 10 percent during the subprime crisis, as opposed to 25 percent during the Great Depression.

GLOBALIZATION

Today more than ever, business leaders, authorities, workers, and families in every country must be aware of the links between their economy and the rest of the world. This chapter describes the process of *globalization* and its macroeconomic implications.

We begin by analyzing the process of globalization and how it has transformed the world. For this analysis, we segment the globalization process into four fundamental components: an increase in international trade, an increase in financial flows across borders, greater *internationalization of production* processes, and the *harmonization of economic institutions*. We then discuss the pros and cons, the benefits and challenges that globalization poses for developing countries. Although this ongoing discussion involves a wide array of economists, in this chapter we present the main views that stand behind the posture in favor of globalization and the one against it.

The Process of Globalization

Globalization is more than an expression or a cliché. The term summarizes an important qualitative change operating in the world economy that affects many aspects of people's lives and the economic policies of nations. Globalization is the economic integration of countries around the world. When one thinks about "economic integration," the first thing that comes to mind is usually international trade, but globalization is much more than that.

Globalization has occurred at least since Europe and China were engaged in long-distance trade in the times of the Roman and Han Empires. Throughout history, and with the discovery of new continents and new forms of communication, trade worldwide has gradually increased.

However, its true apogee began in the nineteenth century, with the *Industrial Revolution*, which was initiated, among other causes, by the use of steam in industrial processes and the spread of railroads.

Figure 6 shows the volume of global exports as a fraction of world GDP, between 1870 and 2016. The figure illustrates that prior to 1929, trade volumes increased, then

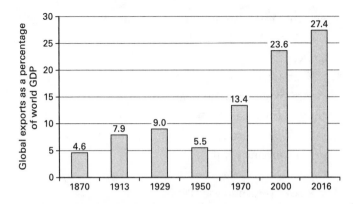

Figure 6 Global exports as a percentage of World GDP, 1870–2016. *Source:* World Bank, *World Development Indicators 2018.*

declined for some time after 1929 (reaching a similar level to that of 1870), and picked up again around 1970 to increase at an even faster pace than before 1929.

Why was there such a setback in the period between the 1930s and the 1960s? The main hypothesis is that the Great Depression—the generalized fall in world output that occurred after 1929—led most countries to increase protection levels, raising *tariffs* (import taxes) and imposing *nontariff barriers*, to limit the exposure of their economies to international fluctuations. In addition, the two world wars and their aftermath meant severe obstacles to international exchanges.

As people increasingly believed that an increase in trade and financial flows improved the overall welfare of their economies, barriers began to gradually diminish and, as of 1970, the volume of international trade increased significantly.

Next we analyze each of the four mentioned components of globalization: increased international trade, increased financial flows across borders, greater internationalization of production processes, and the harmonization of economic institutions.

The Rise of International Trade

There is no doubt that the connections between countries established through international trade have been strongest in the half century since the end of World War II. As evidence, the volume of world trade has grown faster than world GDP in almost every year since 1960. Moreover, the global trade to GDP ratio reached a peak of 61.5 percent in 2008, then fell by almost 10 percent in 2009 as a result of the global recession. However, international trade recovered and has remained above 55 percent of world GDP since 2010.

At least three reasons explain the rapid growth of trade. The first is the progressive elimination of trade barriers during the period after World War II, as a reversal of the trend of trade reduction between 1914 and 1945. After World War I (1914–1918), the Great Depression (1929), and World War II (1939–1945), many countries were closed to trade.

The second reason for the rapid growth of international trade is technological progress. The advances in transportation have been enormous. For instance, air and sea transport have become less expensive and much more reliable, aided by great innovation progress in the area (demonstrated by the use of standardized containers and computer logistics systems). These developments brought dramatic reductions in the costs of transporting goods and passengers. Such technological advances, once novel and now commonplace, reduced the costs of international trade by at least 70 percent, leading to a major rise in the volume of trade.

The third reason is politics and the growing adherence to the idea that trade integration is an engine of development. After World War II, countries were irreconcilably divided into political and economic blocs, with the rich market economies such as the United States, Western Europe, and Japan (or "first world" countries) operating separately from socialist nations such as the Soviet Union, Eastern Europe, and China (referred to as "second world" countries) and from many postcolonial countries, which were referred to as nonaligned (or "third world" countries). The sharp divisions between these groups began to fade in the 1970s and by the 1990s had virtually disappeared. The terminology of "first world" and "third world" is still used, however, to refer to industrialized and emerging or developing countries, respectively.

The Increase in International Capital Flows

Equally notable is the liberalization of *international capital flows*. As occurred with merchandise trade, the international flow of capital collapsed with World War I and recovered at a slow pace afterward. In this case, the conflict was followed by the instability of the 1920s and the Great Depression in the 1930s.

At the end of World War II, the architects of the international economic system of the postwar period—economists such as John Maynard Keynes—made serious efforts to reactivate international trade, but not the international flows of private capital. There was a prevailing feeling that the international mobility of capital was more a source of instability than of prosperity.

However, the postwar economic boom that took place in the United States, Europe, and Japan eventually restored confidence in international loans and, more recently, in foreign investment. By the early 1970s the developing countries of Latin America and Asia saw that they were able to attract loans from international banks and wealthy individuals from advanced countries, flows that were reversed following the *debt crisis* of the 1980s.

During the 1990s, international capital flows increased at an even faster rate than international trade, which in turn grew faster than world GDP. The rapid growth of capital flows in the world is presented in figure 7, which also shows a sharp drop in international financial transactions in 2001 as a result of the slowdown in the main developed countries and the greater political uncertainty generated by terrorism. Uncertainty also increased sharply with the subprime crisis as expectations fell and investors' appetite for risk decreased, leading capital flows to drastically decrease in 2009.

The recent evolution of private capital flows has been very different from that of international trade. Figure 7 shows that the current levels are more similar to those observed at the beginning of the 1990s, and much lower than those reached in 2007. The most permanent change in the level of international capital flows is partially explained by a change of mentality and regulation. Prior to the crisis, there was widespread confidence in the benefits of financial innovation and its ability to transfer risk to the agents most adept at managing it, as well as a preference for the self-regulation of markets over state intervention. With the global financial crisis of 2008, this position has evolved toward a more cautious mentality in the financial world, sustained by the belief that without proper regulation, markets are prone to the creation of *bubbles,* that excessive leverage (or too much debt in relation to equity) generates *systemic risk*, that the lack of transparency undermines trust, and that early intervention in a deregulated market is preferable to late intervention since the costs and damages will most likely be smaller. This position leads to more regulated financial markets and greater

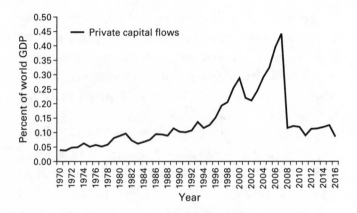

Figure 7 Private capital flows (% of GDP), 1970–2016. *Source:* World Bank, *World Development Indicators 2018*; International Monetary Fund, *International Financial Statistics,* 2018.

caution in the financial risks assumed, which is reflected in a moderation of capital flows.

The increase in international capital flows is associated with opportunities and risks. To some extent, the opportunities were highlighted in the growth observed between the 1990s and the early 2000s. On the other hand, the risks and consequences were clearly seen in the aftermath of the Asian crisis in the late 1990s (after which capital flows recovered only after 2002) and later with the subprime crisis in 2008.

Foreign direct investment (FDI), which is the purchase of controlling stakes by investors of one country in a business in another country, contributes with funds, newer technology, and sometimes more efficient management. This arrangement benefits the companies and developing countries receiving FDI by providing them with greater opportunities for growth. However, in terms of risks, the increase in short-term international loans is accompanied by periods of high volatility.

These risks materialized in both the Asian crisis and the subprime crisis, when FDI was a big source of foreign capital during the boom of private capital flows. The volatility brought on by these surges of capital flows lead to debtors' situations changing overnight. All of a sudden, people could no longer take out loans, and those indebted were forced to make large payments. Obviously, a great majority of these debtors were unable to pay, leading to a series of debt defaults, which resulted in the collapse of the financial system. Hence the controversy over the benefits and costs of the international mobility of capital.

The Internationalization of Production

A subtler if no less remarkable manifestation of globalization than the increase in international trade and capital flows is the internationalization of production. A typical capital or consumption good is simultaneously national and foreign if one part was produced in the country and another part produced abroad. It is quite common to find sophisticated goods such as computers or automobiles with components coming from more than a dozen nations. Even clothes are sometimes processed among several countries: one produces the fiber, another processes the fabric, a third country designs the item, and a fourth country may be in charge of the cutting and making, before the item ends up in a store in a fifth country.

The result is an increasingly globalized production system. Production by multinational organizations represents a large and increasing proportion of the total merchandise that is produced and traded. In a globalized production system, each company evaluates which parts of the good are best produced at home and which ones are most conveniently produced abroad. In general, such a consideration is heavily influenced by the cost of production factors in the different potential supplier markets. Insofar as salaries are considerably lower in most developing countries than in advanced economies, it makes sense to carry out the labor-intensive parts of the production process in a developing nation, leaving procedures that are intensive in capital or technology for more advanced economies.

Globalized production has existed for centuries as large companies have maintained subsidiaries abroad to ensure the supply of basic inputs. But the spread of globalized production systems has grown tremendously over the past thirty years. Globalized production would have not scaled up so quickly if it had not been for the incredibly high speed of technological growth and constant improvement, in addition to decreasing international barriers to trade and growing international collaboration.

The internationalization of production changed the economic growth strategy of developing countries forever. Some fifty to one hundred years ago, Latin American and Asian countries specialized almost entirely in agricultural or mining production and exported to international markets, using the proceeds to purchase manufactured goods from advanced economies. With the globalization of production, some successful developing countries found a quite different niche in the global economy. As a result, they are now part of the international high-tech merchandise production chain, producing components of complex final goods, which are then sold all over the world. Countries such as these (e.g., China, India, and Brazil) attract investment from large multinational corporations in Europe, the United States, and Japan. As a result, local production has been transformed into another stage of the international production system.

A successful strategy in some developing countries is to establish export processing zones (EPZs). The EPZs are areas that offer incentives and an environment of reduced barriers to attract foreign investment to local production and in this way promote economic growth. EPZs may sometimes offer facilities for transport, communications, energy supply, or even favorable tax treatments (e.g., lower tax rates). In developing countries, where, for instance, transport and communication may be hindered by the lack of good roads or reliable internet access, where perhaps safety is not guaranteed and robberies or kidnapping may be frequent, or where bureaucracy and excessive required paperwork may obstruct the ease of doing business, setting up an EPZ may be useful in attracting multinational organizations to carry out local productive operations.

The Harmonization of Economic Institutions

In addition to an increase in trade, finance, and international production, when becoming globalized, national governments make the conscious decision to harmonize their economic institutions so that the "rules of the game" are increasingly similar throughout the world. Harmonization of economic institutions implies the creation of a "level playing field" for equivalent economic institutions around the world. In this way, the cost of doing business with the rest of the world is reduced and the advantages of international economic integration increase. International economic institutions, such as the *International Monetary Fund*, the *World Bank*, the European Central Bank, and the *World Trade Organization*, among others, play an important role.

The International Monetary Fund (IMF) is an organization of 189 member countries that works to encourage the development of global monetary cooperation, secure financial stability, facilitate international trade, promote high employment and sustainable economic growth, and reduce poverty around the world. It was conceived at a UN conference in Bretton Woods, New Hampshire, in 1944, where representatives of forty-four countries gathered after World War II to attempt to establish a new world order and build a framework for economic cooperation to avoid situations similar to the one that led to the Great Depression of the 1930s.

The World Bank also had its origins in 1944 at the Bretton Woods Conference. It has expanded to a group (the World Bank Group) of five development institutions: the International Bank for Reconstruction and Development (IBRD), the International Development Association (IDA), the International Finance Corporation (IFC), the Multilateral Investment Guarantee Agency (MIGA), and the International Center for Settlement of Investment Disputes (ICSID). Originally, the World Bank's loans helped rebuild countries devastated by World War II. Eventually the focus shifted from reconstruction to development, with a heavy emphasis on infrastructure such as dams, irrigation systems, and roads. Today the IBRD and the IDA provide financing, policy advice, and technical assistance to governments of developing countries. The IDA focuses on the world's poorest countries, while the IBRD assists middle-income and creditworthy poorer countries. However, the World Bank Group as a whole is committed to reducing poverty, supporting economic growth, and ensuring sustainable gains in the quality of people's lives.

The World Trade Organization (WTO) was established in 1995 as a successor to the General Agreement on Tariffs and Trade (GATT), which was created in 1947 at a UN conference as a legal agreement between many countries; its overall purpose was to promote international trade by reducing or eliminating trade barriers such as tariffs or quotas. The WTO provides a forum for negotiating agreements to reduce the obstacles to international trade and to ensure a level playing field for all countries. The WTO also provides a legal and institutional framework for the implementation and monitoring of these agreements, as well as for settling disputes that may arise from their interpretation and application.

What do institutions such as these do to create a level playing field? For example, in 1995, the WTO propelled the Agreement on Trade-Related Aspects of Intellectual Property Rights (TRIPS), an international legal agreement between all the member nations of the WTO that set out general principles for the enforcement of intellectual property rights (i.e., copyrights, patents, and trademarks). This agreement is extremely important to guarantee fair conditions in global trade. On the other hand, the World Bank in 2013 began an Agricultural Productivity Program for Southern Africa to increase the availability of improved agricultural technologies. The World Bank fosters many programs, such as this one, that provide financing and assistance to the region that is being helped. And as we saw in previous chapters, the IMF provides many other types of loans, including those to support structural adjustment programs in the poorest countries, help in stabilization programs, and assist in the management of certain external debt crises. An example is the creation in 1963 of the Compensatory Financing Facility (CFF), a credit fund explicitly designed to lend to countries experiencing temporary declines in their exports, which was slightly modified in 1988, transforming it into the Compensatory and Contingency Financing Facility (CCFF), to broaden its range of action beyond the event of a fall in exports.

The next section delves into the crises that have occurred in the era of globalization, their causes, and the role of multilateral institutions.

Crises, Globalization, and the Role of Multilateral Institutions

Various global agreements and efforts at coordination have emerged in response to wars and crises. One such was the United Nations Monetary and Financial Conference, convened at Bretton Woods in July 1944, toward the end of World War II, to discuss the pillars of a new world economic order. The IMF and World Bank were created at this conference to provide institutional assistance for global recovery from the war and to prevent unstable situations such as the one that led to the Great Depression of the 1930s.

Another example of global agreement and coordination in answer to global crises is the *Washington Consensus,* which emerged after the debt crisis of the 1980s. The crisis was sparked by Mexico's declaration that it would cease making payment on its debts (*debt moratorium*) in 1982. This caused a massive flight of capital and the emergence of negative expectations that quickly spread to the rest of Latin America, with a consequent restriction on access to international credit, large recessions, currency devaluations, and increases in inflation. The consequences of the debt crisis of the 1980s were so serious that by the end of the 1980s, the affected countries had barely managed to recover to the levels of GDP per capita they had at the beginning of the decade, a situation that gave rise to the expression *lost decade*. The crisis also spread to Africa and Asia, though it was shorter in Asia. After this episode, several specialists met in Washington to elaborate a set of policy recommendations whose objective was to avoid future crises in developing countries. The product of this work is known as the Washington Consensus. The consensus was adopted by the main multilateral organizations (e.g., the

IMF, the World Bank, and the US Treasury Department) and was considered important to stabilizing the global economy. As part of the consensus, it was agreed that granting loans to developing countries hit by the crisis would be conditional on those countries meeting certain goals or policy prescriptions. The prescriptions, or reform plans, were designed to help the recovery of developing markets hit by the crisis and included, for instance, macroeconomic stabilization policies and economic openness policies in trade and investment.

Joseph Stiglitz, professor at Columbia University, former chief economist at the World Bank, and 2001 winner of the Nobel Prize in Economics, is well known for his negative opinions about globalization. He has pointed out that rather than preventing global financial crises, as these measures were intended to do, globalization (particularly of capital flows) imposed on developing countries as a condition for the granting of credit lines from the IMF and the World Bank was the cause of the crisis in Mexico in 1994, the Asian crisis in 1997–1998, the Russian crisis in 1998, the crisis in Brazil in 1999, the crisis in Argentina in 2001, and the subprime mortgage crisis in the United States 2008. Many of his most trenchant views are presented in books published in 2002 and 2006.

A more accurate look at the actions of such organisms would help to understand this point of view. Broadly speaking, a typical IMF or World Bank aid program includes the beneficiary country's obligation to execute a four-step plan: privatize, liberalize capital flows, liberalize price controls, and open markets to international trade. Privatizations seek to reduce the size of the state, which would be expected to make it more efficient and eliminate some of the usual sources of fiscal deficits. The *liberalization of capital flows* (i.e., the reduction of barriers to the movement of capital across borders) is essential for any developing country to access the international markets and obtain resources. The liberalization of domestic prices implies determining prices according to supply and demand in a market-based system, which is much more efficient than a system of controlled prices. Finally, trade openness promotes competition and efficiency and is an important channel for the transmission of knowledge and new technologies.

In practice, however, these policies do not always produce the desired results. Privatization sometimes generates corruption, as was the case in Russia in 1995, when, facing a severe fiscal deficit and in desperate need of funds, the Russian government adopted a scheme whereby some of the largest state industrial assets were sold though auction at very low prices to favored insiders with political connections. Opening the capital account allows the free flow of capital or resources for speculative purposes, which resources arrive in good times and escape massively in bad times: this happened during the main crises of the

1990s and the Great Recession that started in late 2008, as well as during the 1994 Mexican crisis, discussed in chapter 5, which saw a sudden reversal of capital flows. In the case of Mexico, although the rescue package delivered by multilateral organizations has been considered a key factor in the rapid recovery of the country, others say the true reason was the recovery of imports of Mexican products by its North America Free Trade Agreement (NAFTA) trading partners (i.e., the picking up of Mexican exports). On the other hand, the spread of this crisis to other emerging economies, such as Argentina in 1995, underlined the risks of globalization in terms of contagion, which reoccurred during the 1997 Asian crisis and the 2008–2009 subprime mortgage crisis. The liberalization of domestic prices can, in turn, cause social unrest, as occurred in Indonesia in 1998, when the IMF led a program to eliminate subsidies for food and gasoline.

The critical vision has solid foundations in some specific cases, but not in general. There are very hasty liberalizations and privatizations without clear rules of the game and with poor legal frameworks, or simply riddled with corruption, which undermines the success of these programs. Nevertheless, there are many examples of privatization carried out with transparency and under an efficient legal framework, as well as examples of a well-regulated opening of the financial sector with a healthy banking sector, the liberalization of prices and reduction of distortions in decentralized markets, and trade liberalization after the release of domestic prices. These results are usually the prelude to an important leap in the development of nations. Such was the case, for example, with East Germany after the fall of the Berlin Wall, when the economy was suddenly exposed to the economic model of the West. Much was invested into the rehabilitation of the former East Germany in helping it transition to a market economy. However, this process is never easy, and in the case of Germany it required several serious negotiations that culminated in a Unification Treaty. Although efforts focused on a speedy reunification process, complications abounded. For example, there was much confusion over property rights: many enterprises had been first expropriated by the Nazis and later privatized after the fall of the Berlin Wall. It took many political cycles of negotiations to establish clear and efficient legal frameworks.

The Arguments against Globalization

Globalization brings undeniable progress and well-being for a large majority, but it also generates social changes and inequality, which cannot be ignored. The frequent popular demonstrations against globalization during meetings of international organizations such as the World Bank, the

World Economic Forum, the IMF, and the World Trade Organization, among others, are a sign of growing discomfort arising from the problems and inequalities associated with global development. This was evident in 2016 in the United Kingdom at the beginning of its attempts to exit from the EU (the *Brexit* process).

The antiglobalization movement is sustained by a feeling of an inequitable distribution of the benefits of globalization and the centralized decision-making involved. However, since the impact of economic integration is difficult to quantify, often the positive effects of globalization on the quality of people's lives are not appropriately considered. The positive effects of globalization (which we discuss later in the chapter) may include the availability of a wider variety of products, lower prices, possibly products of better quality, and greater job opportunities. Foreign investment may push local authorities to improve infrastructure (e.g., telephony, antennas, and roads), further benefiting citizens.

Joseph Stiglitz has said that globalization, in principle, has the potential to generate benefits, particularly for developing countries, when policies are applied properly—that is, when they take into account the individual conditions and characteristics of each nation. In practice, globalization has generated benefits such as higher economic development through increased trade, improved access to knowledge and technologies, and the removal of several developing countries from isolation. However, for Stiglitz, the benefits have coexisted with a worsening of living conditions in most developing countries in tandem with an increase in world income. Furthermore, he considers these economies economically unstable, as shown by the financial crises that occurred in Asia and Latin America in the late 1990s and by the subprime crisis that began in 2008. According to Stiglitz, the governing bodies of the "new world order" (the IMF, the World Bank, and the WTO) are to blame for dogmatically applying programs to "alleviate" problems in developing countries, but with insufficient transparency and with disastrous results most of the time.

This critique focuses on two fundamental components of globalization, international trade and international capital flows. For Stiglitz, the terms on which free trade has been implemented are not fair: while developing countries are required to open the economy to the industrial products of developed countries, the latter (essentially the EU and the United States) subsidize their own agricultural production, preventing developing countries from selling their products to those developed countries. The developing world's inability to compete ultimately destroys regional agricultural economies, leading to greater poverty and unemployment.

Another criticism is that policies aimed at liberalizing financial systems would have generated more difficult access to credit for small local businesses since many of the banks in developing countries were acquired by foreign banks, which in turn would have greater incentives to lend money to large companies than to small or medium-sized enterprises. In addition, the argument goes, the liberalization of capital markets has generated greater global instability characterized by the reversal in capital flows to emerging countries.

According to Stiglitz, the development of the subprime crisis, the contagion to Europe, and the consequent beginning of the euro crisis would not have been possible were it not for the failures in the design of the monetary union of the euro. Moreover, dissatisfaction with globalization can be exemplified by the Brexit referendum in 2016, where a majority of voters in the UK agreed that the benefits of being a member of the EU were less than the costs. Some of the "leave" campaign's arguments addressed topics such as immigration, energy, and the environment. For example, those in favor of Brexit said that public services were under strain because of the number of migrants, that high immigration rates had driven down the wages of the British workers, and that it was impossible to control immigration so long as the UK was a member of the EU. People also believed that EU environmental regulation was an unnecessary burden on business and pushed up energy prices. The UK's overall dissatisfaction with EU membership may have been attributed to a poorly designed EU and an all too rigid and flawed euro zone, where there are no tailored responses to individual members' issues. We return to Brexit at the end of this chapter.

Another important critic of globalization is George Soros, investor, business magnate, philanthropist, political activist, and author. Instead of referring to a "global economy," he uses the term "global capitalist system," whose great deficiencies are an unequal income distribution, an unstable financial system, the threat of global monopolies (among other forms of market organization that are not competitive), the diminished power of the state, and the weakening of values and social cohesion.

A central element in Soros's critique is "market fundamentalism," which may be defined as the general agreement that markets work well and automatically correct themselves when out of equilibrium, that the best way to serve common interests is by allowing each person to individually defend his or her own interests, and that any intervention distorts the market. To Soros, this fundamentalism is the reason why the global capitalist system is unsustainable. Furthermore, he says that free market performance leads to imbalance, which may be illustrated by the burst of the housing bubble (preceded by market deregulation and financial innovations), ending in the 2009 recession.

According to him, when the imbalances generated by the market affect society, the state must intervene. This is a key element to his argument. He says that, while the economy has globalized, society and the state have not. Ultimately, then, according to Soros, we have a global economy without having a global society in which common well-being is more important than individual interests.

The Case for Globalization

Other authors have argued in favor of globalization and have tried to measure its benefits. One of them is Xavier Sala-i-Martin, who in works published in 2006 and 2016 evaluates the effects of globalization on poverty and income inequality. According to him, these are the two most important phenomena of the second half of the twentieth century.

Evidence shows that there is a tight relationship between economic growth and poverty: countries with faster income per capita growth (faster than a 3 percent annual growth rate, according to some studies) are also countries where trade has grown significantly. The divergent paths of Asia and Africa in poverty reduction illustrate this point. China adopted a market economy in 1978 (after Mao's death) and, having had higher poverty rates than Africa up until the early 1990s, began to reduce poverty at a pace never seen before in history, reaching poverty rates below Africa's as soon as 1993 and below the world average by

2005. Meanwhile, Africa has also reduced poverty, but at a much slower pace than other more globalized regions, and still has a notably high poverty rate.

Figure 8 shows the *extreme poverty* rates for the main world regions, that is, the percentage of the population that lives on less than $1.90 per day. The graph shows that extreme poverty has decreased considerably in Asia and to a lesser extent in Latin America and the Middle East.

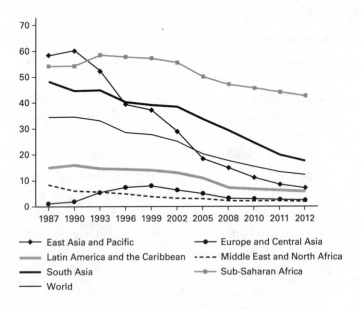

Figure 8 Extreme poverty in selected regions (% of total population).
Source: Roser and Ortiz-Ospina, "Global Extreme Poverty."

Similar conclusions can be drawn when analyzing the number of people living in poverty in these regions. In 1960, China and India harbored the largest number of poor people on the planet. However, the spectacular performance of Asia, reflected in its high growth rates, and the poor performance of Africa have meant that poverty has gone from being an essentially Asian phenomenon to being a phenomenon concentrated mainly in the African continent. Despite the above observations, in global terms, both the poverty rate and the number of people living in poverty have decreased over time.

One of the most common ways of calculating income inequality is by using the *Gini coefficient*, as we show in figure 9. The Gini coefficient fluctuates between 0 and 1, where 0 corresponds to a totally equitable distribution and 1 corresponds to a scenario of complete inequality (one person has all the income and the rest have none). Considered from a long-term perspective, and in global terms, inequality has slightly declined: the global Gini measure went from 0.72 to 0.70 in twenty years. However, in certain short periods of time, inequality may increase.

According to Sala-i-Martin, the conclusion is clear: from a global and long-term perspective, inequality has decreased since 1980, and the reason for this is that once the economies of China and India began to open up to the world and to accept the process of globalization, they achieved high growth rates, joining countries in the region

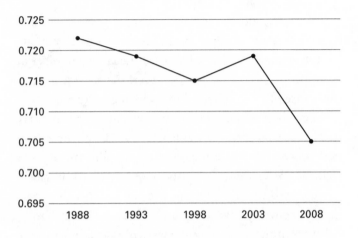

Figure 9 Measures of world income distribution: global Gini index. *Source:* Lakner and Milanovic, "Global Income Distribution."

with high performance such as South Korea, Malaysia, Thailand, Singapore, and Indonesia. Therefore, more than half of the world population began to grow; in many cases, it grew at rates of more than 6 percent per year, and several times it exceeded 10 percent. That is, there was a rapid convergence on the part of some of the poorest countries toward the level of the richest countries. And that, in short, is the reason why inequality has been reduced in the world.

New Views on Globalization

Other authors have studied the possibility that globalization has different effects, depending on the income level of people. This view was presented by Christopher Lakner and Branko Milanovic in 2013 in a graph that was quickly dubbed the "elephant curve" of global inequality; the curve illustrates the real changes in the income of people according to their percentile in the global income distribution between 1988 and 2008. The vertical axis shows the growth rate of income between 1988 and 2008 while the horizontal axis shows the level of income in 1988 (relative to the income distribution of the entire world in 1988). This graph, shown in figure 10, supports the idea that globalization has been more positive (upward-trending curve) in increasing the wealth of some people more than others. The most favored have been those belonging to the emerging global middle class (China and India, mainly in the fiftieth percentile), along with the richest people in the richest countries (hundredth percentile). Those negatively affected in these thirty years, according to the graph, belong to the working classes of the richest countries (upper middle class, between the seventy-fifth and ninetieth percentiles of the global income distribution), who have seen negative growth in their real income, while for the poorest (those in sub-Saharan Africa and elsewhere, in the lowest fifth percentile of the distribution), real income

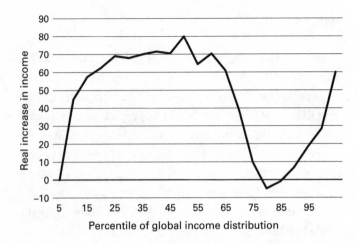

Figure 10 Change in real income between 1988 and 2008 at various percentiles of global income distribution (calculated in 2005 international dollars). *Source:* Milanovic, *Global Inequality.*

remains almost unchanged. The analysis also reveals that, although income inequality between countries has decreased, it has increased within them.

This analysis by income groups may explain much of the dissatisfaction expressed in the UK's referendum on Brexit, the results of the 2016 US presidential election, and the growing emergence of populist movements and nationalism in Europe. According to Milanovic, the lack of a more equitable redistribution of the gains of globalization has pushed the emergence of "deglobalizing" forces. The main concern of the rich countries is the stagnation of incomes of the middle classes. Another concern is that the rise of populism is based mainly on the perception that Asia—mainly China—is prospering at the expense of the West.

The Need for International Cooperation: Currency and Trade Wars

A better understanding of the globalization process and its effects on people's living standards is fundamental to addressing the current criticism and avoiding populist responses to complex economic problems. Along the same lines, increased international cooperation is required to sustain an open global economy and to increase people's gains from it. Among the multiple global challenges, currency and trade wars represent two latent threats that should be avoided by the international community.

Currency wars occur when countries try to deliberately depreciate exchange rates to gain a competitive advantage. A weaker currency means a country's exports are cheaper, which makes local production more attractive than its competitors' production overseas. In simple terms, if the Mexican peso loses value with respect to the Brazilian real, then one US dollar will buy more in Mexico than it will in Brazil, which means that for a US resident, it will be cheaper to import the same item from Mexico. Any

Currency wars occur
when countries try to
deliberately depreciate
exchange rates to gain a
competitive advantage.

country may be tempted to seek this competitive advantage; however, it is likely that trade partners will respond in a similar way, ending up with large currency interventions and a negative effect on global trade.

In 2010, when the US dollar was depreciating against emerging market currencies, China prevented this from happening to its currency, thus leading to a conflict between China and the United States. Because the exchange rate between the Chinese and the US currencies moved very little, the US dollar depreciation was assimilated to a greater extent in other emerging markets, such as Brazil, Chile, Colombia, and Mexico. Facing large appreciation pressures, the affected emerging markets also began to take protective measures, such as imposing capital controls, accumulating reserves, or reducing government spending. Although this conflict never reached uncontrollable levels, it serves as a clear example of how a currency conflict between two countries can easily escalate to becoming a global issue.

Trade wars and protectionist policies follow a similar logic to currency wars. To boost domestic industries, a country may be tempted to impose higher tariffs on imported products, which reduces competition for local producers. However, this will most likely give way to a similar response from its trade partners, resulting in larger tariffs, diminished international trade, and a reduction in global economic growth.

The trade tensions between China and the United States that began in 2018 may be illustrative of the potential economic costs of a trade war. When the conflict started, global growth projections for upcoming years gradually were reduced. In fact, the IMF estimated that, if all the protectionist announcements were materialized, there would be permanent and significant negative growth effects for China, the United States, the emerging economies, and the world as a whole. In the end, there are no winners in a trade war.

Brexit and Globalization

The UK held a referendum on whether to leave or stay in the EU on June 23, 2016. The discussion was mainly focused on immigration, crime, trade, sovereignty, and the economic and financial importance of the UK within the EU. The supporters of the "leave" campaign felt that the UK would benefit in these respects by leaving the EU. In terms of immigration, they said that the UK would never have real control over immigration into its territory as long as it was the EU authorities that dictated the movements to and from member countries; in economic and financial terms, those who supported Brexit said that London was the main financial center of the EU. Based on these arguments, many saw Brexit as a clear manifestation of discontent with globalization.

Sala-i-Martin has said that the EU is not truly democratic; as evidence, he notes in a 2016 blog post that the leadership of the European Commission and the European Council is not democratically elected but nevertheless makes decisions that affect all the countries of the EU. He explains that recent nationalist and protectionist movements have a common origin in the discontent brought on by globalization. More concretely, the transfer of the centers of manufacturing production to China, India, and Vietnam, the loss of industrial jobs in the West, and the new industrial revolution (characterized by digitalization, robotics, artificial intelligence, nanotechnology, big data) have had the world's middle class among its main losers.

Recalling that the last time the world was *"deglobalized"* was at the beginning of the twentieth century—culminating in World War II—Sala-i-Martin reveals a common concern to many observing the rapid growth of followers of a new antiglobalization movement. Although the manifestation of this discontent has been most striking in the last few years, many had much earlier begun asking themselves, from a more technical perspective, how much globalization is good.

An example is Dani Rodrik, who in his 2010 book, *The Globalization Paradox: Democracy and the Future of the*

World Economy, asks whether perhaps the world has taken globalization too far, or whether it should at least question its pros and cons. He reflects on the sustainability of global capitalism, in a context in which developing countries claim that the system is biased against their interests because it is the rich and most influential countries that make the rules.

The discussion is not nearly over. Globalization has pros and cons. However, research tends to support the point of view that globalization has achieved higher living standards. Nevertheless, the roots of discontent regarding globalization should not be overlooked. The answer may be in suggesting different growth paths for different countries and regions. For example, cultural differences should be heavily considered, along with history, institutions, laws, and the degree of political corruption. Differences in characteristics such as these allow authorities (local or global) to take into account the complexity of change and how this affects the wide array of possible outcomes in development.

In the end, although societies are likely to prosper as a whole with globalization, there always will be winners and losers. Public policies should take care of those less favored by globalization through education, training programs, job conversion, and, in extreme cases, government aid. Widely spreading the benefits of globalization is, therefore, one of the fundamental challenges of societies today.

CONCLUSION

Macroeconomics provides answers to many of the most pressing questions that countries, organizations, and families face in day-to-day life. Throughout the eleven chapters of this book we have learned about several topics: the overall level of production (GDP) and its relation to the welfare of people; the sources of economic growth, and why some countries grow strongly while others stagnate; the challenges of the labor market in the twenty-first century and the measurements of unemployment; the money market and the inflation rate; the implications of having different exchange rate systems—fixed, pegged, bands, or floating; household consumption and saving decisions; investment decisions; the current account of the balance of payments; the government budget, taxes, and fiscal policy; and the exciting debate over globalization, its effects on people's well-being, and how these effects relate to the recent protectionist dynamics seen in some developed countries.

In discussing these topics, we have reviewed the most relevant economic theories, evidence, and phenomena of recent times and analyzed the factors that explain the development of nations. We have also looked at recent economic crises, such as the subprime crisis and the subsequent euro crisis, addressing their causes and consequences.

By now, the reader has most likely acquired knowledge of the main elements and basic forces that govern each country's economy and the global economy. This knowledge is vital to the decisions made by policymakers, households and businesses in a globalized world.

Let us go through the main topics we have addressed.

The most important measurement of an economy is the gross domestic product. This concept tries to measure the total value of the goods and services produced within the geographic limits of a country or region in a specific period and is often interpreted as a measure of overall economic welfare. However, there are several limitations to traditional measures of well-being such as the GDP, and throughout the years, complementary measures have been developed, such as the Human Development Index and the World Happiness Index. Regardless of the measure, the reader has most likely realized by now how important overall economic growth is for individual and national well-being.

Economic growth in a specific country can be achieved by a greater accumulation of productive factors, capital, and labor or through technological innovation. In either case, growth is heavily influenced by saving and investment decisions, which in turn are greatly determined by economic policies such as the degree of openness to foreign trade, political and economic institutions such as an independent central bank, a fiscal rule, and sometimes even by geographic features. Which of these elements is more relevant for economic growth is still controversial and often specific to countries and periods of time.

The fact that a strong and healthy labor market spurs economic growth, and vice versa, defines the close relationship between GDP and the labor market. Perhaps the main indicator of the labor market is the unemployment rate, which measures the percentage of the population that is actively looking for a job without finding one. The unemployment rate is also related to the flexibility of the labor market: markets where labor flows freely, that is, where there are few obstacles to the hiring and dismissal of workers, have lower unemployment rates than those with strict regulations. However, the unemployment rate has some weaknesses as a measure of a healthy labor market as it does not capture, for instance, the quality of work and is influenced by the number of people who have been frustrated in their attempts to be hired and have ceased looking for jobs. The first issue is addressed by measures of underemployment; the second issue is denoted the "discouraged worker effect."

We then analyzed inflation, its relation to money and economic activity, and how monetary authorities regulate the circulation of money. The rate of inflation measures the percentage change in the general level of prices of goods and services in an economy. Over time, the fluctuations in prices raise important issues, especially related to:

the cost of living, as higher inflation makes living more expensive; the management of monetary policy, where the monetary authority's responsibility is to stabilize inflation mainly through the monetary policy interest rate (its monetary policy tool); and the difficulty of stabilizing rates of inflation that are too low or too high where activity is hard to boost back to healthy levels.

A closely related issue is the role of the exchange rate and the different exchange rate regimes, which may be flexible (floating), fixed (pegged), or intermediate. In a flexible exchange rate system, the exchange rate is determined by the supply of and demand for domestic and foreign currency, whereas in a fixed exchange rate system, a currency's value is fixed against the value of another currency (e.g., the US dollar or the euro), to a basket of currencies, or to the value of another asset (e.g., gold or silver). After learning a bit of this, we were able to understand what drove Ecuador, El Salvador, and Zimbabwe to dollarize in 2000, 2001, and 2009, respectively; what led Argentina to abandon its currency board and adopt a flotation scheme in 2002; and the implications for European countries of adopting the euro in 1999.

The main components of GDP are consumption, investment, and government spending. Consumption basically measures households' expenditure on goods and services that have no productive purpose for the long term (otherwise the expenditure would be considered an investment) and is fundamental to understanding how an economy works. In fact, it is the main component of GDP; that is, most of national production goes to satisfy the consumption needs of people.

Physical investment is the accumulation of capital in the form of machinery, equipment, and buildings. Adding the study of investment to the analysis of consumption allows us to better understand how production is distributed in each period between its current use (consumption) and its future use (investment to accumulate capital and increase future consumption). In addition, fluctuations in business investment play a central role in determining the level of output and employment in the short run; thus they have a crucial role in the business cycle. Investment also contributes significantly to long-term economic growth.

Another key variable for macroeconomists is the current account of the balance of payments, which measures the exports of goods and services from one country to the rest of the world, minus its imports of goods and services from the rest of the world, plus the net transfers that the country receives from abroad. In general terms, when a country's income is greater than its consumption, there is a surplus in its current account. Conversely, when consumption is greater than income, the country has a current account deficit.

Key concepts related to the current account are a country's trade balance and international financial flows.

The trade balance is an important component of the current account: it measures the difference between a country's imports (which are part of its consumption and investment) and its exports (which are an important part of its production). International capital flows are financial movements across borders. In general terms, when a country imports more goods and services than it exports, residents of that country must pay for such imports, either by borrowing from other countries or by reducing their holdings of foreign assets. On the other hand, when exports exceed imports, the country's residents are generally lending to the rest of the world or increasing their holdings of foreign assets.

We then moved on to analyzing fiscal policy and its macroeconomic effects. The basic point here is that prudent fiscal policy that leads to low deficits (or in some cases surpluses) and moderate levels of public debt is an essential component of macroeconomic stability and thus of an economic environment conducive to long-term growth. In contrast, excess fiscal spending may lead to large fiscal deficits and an accumulation of public debt, fueling a vicious and unsustainable cycle that could result in the government's inability to pay its debt (default), which would have severe effects on the economy. Fiscal policy should aim at being countercyclical (moving contrary to the direction of the economic cycle) rather than procyclical (moving in the same direction as the economic cycle). A countercyclical fiscal policy allows fiscal expansion when the overall economy is contracting or barely growing and reduces the rate of growth of fiscal spending when the economy is expanding. Countercyclical fiscal policies are advised as stabilizing mechanisms for the economic cycle. Structural fiscal rules have been implemented by several countries in pursuit of this objective.

Our journey ends with the debate over economic crises and globalization.

The world changed profoundly with the fall of communism in 1989 and with the growing integration of countries into the world economy, especially China and India. Thus the world economy has become truly globalized for the first time in history. Since then, the events of the international economy have been increasingly affecting nations, as evidenced by the so-called Great Recession that started in 2008. This crisis was initially limited to the real estate sector in the United States but quickly moved to its financial sector and then, through international links, to other industrialized economies, and finally became a global issue. As the recession unfolded in many countries, not only did important international banks fail, but many other companies from various sectors were ruined. In terms of employment, millions of people lost their jobs throughout the world.

The globalization process has four fundamental components: an increase in international trade, an increase in financial flows across borders, greater internationalization of production processes, and the harmonization of economic institutions across the world.

While there is evidence that globalization brings undeniable progress and well-being for a large majority of the world, there is also evidence that some countries have reaped greater benefits from it than others, and a few authors have suggested that globalization may even have harmed some countries by increasing their exposure to crises.

This discussion is far from over. Although research tends to support the point of view that globalization has resulted in higher living standards, discontent regarding globalization should not be overlooked. There are certainly many losers from globalization, even in countries that have benefited from it. And, although societies are likely to prosper as a whole with globalization, public policies should focus on compensating the losers and avoiding the emergence of protectionist sentiments.

Achieving a healthy, sustained, and inclusive global growth path is not an easy task. Strong levels of investment and trade, with the collaboration and support of monetary and fiscal policies, fiscal responsibility, stable monetary conditions, strong job growth in a healthy labor market, sustainable levels of private and public indebtedness, and public policies for education and training programs, are some of the most important components of a successful development strategy.

accelerated depreciation
Method of depreciation that allows greater deductions for tax purposes than those corresponding to the useful life of an asset. Accelerated depreciation implies lower taxation after the investment is made.

additional worker effect
An effect that increases the unemployment rate when a member of a household who had not previously sought work begins seeking work upon another household member's loss of work, which would then appear in the unemployment data as two people unemployed rather than one. Compare with *discouraged worker effect*, which manifests as a fall in the unemployment rate.

Asian crisis
A sequence of currency devaluations that began in Thailand in 1997 and rapidly spread to other countries in Southeast Asia. This crisis had meaningful investment and growth effects on several emerging economies well beyond Asia.

Asian tigers
Hong Kong, Singapore, South Korea, and Taiwan, which underwent a rapid industrialization process and maintained exceptionally high growth rates between the early 1960s and the 1990s.

backed money
A currency that is fully convertible into a specific amount of gold, silver, or other commodity.

balance of payments
Macroeconomic account that measures all the transactions of a country with the rest of the world over a certain period of time.

balance of payments crisis
An economic crisis that ensues when the exchange rate system collapses as the central bank faces a progressive depletion of its international reserves, which typically leads to a decline in the value of the country's currency.

Brexit
The expected departure of the United Kingdom from the European Union after a referendum on the matter.

bubble
A market phenomenon characterized by surges in asset prices to levels significantly above the fundamental value of the asset.

central bank autonomy
The independence of a country's central bank from the government, as established by a legal framework. Central bank autonomy increases the bank's credibility as an institution.

central government
Governmental and administrative agencies at the national (federal) level.

classical approach
Traditional economic approach to analyzing the labor and goods markets that assumes complete flexibility of wages and prices, and so wages and prices adjust to maintain the equilibrium between the supply of and demand for labor and the supply of and demand for goods.

closed economy
An economy that does not carry out commercial or financial transactions with the rest of the world.

collateralized debt obligation
A structured financial instrument backed by securities that in turn are backed by credit claims. Some examples are building loans, student loans, and car loans.

consolidated public sector
That part of the economy composed of both public services and public organizations. The consolidated public sector encompasses the nonfinancial public sector (e.g., regional and local governments, national pension funds, state universities, nonfinancial public enterprises) to the central bank and financial institutions owned by the state.

consumer confidence
Mood of consumers with regard to economic conditions such as unemployment, inflation, and expectations about future events. Consumer confidence is normally used to anticipate future economic activity.

consumption
Household consumer expenditures on goods and services.

contagion
The rapid transfer of the effects of an economic crisis in one country to other economies.

cost inflation
Sustained increase in the price level that results from an increase in the cost of productive factors.

cost of capital
The cost of financing an investment project, which is closely related to the interest rate.

countercyclical (fiscal)
Denoting categories of public spending that tend to increase in periods of recession periods and decrease when an economy recovers, thus smoothing a country's economic cycle.

credit crunch
A macroeconomic situation in which banks significantly restrict their credit supply.

credit rationing
The limiting by lenders of credit to borrowers. Not all individuals or companies can freely borrow at the market interest rate to finance their investments (or consumption), even when a project is profitable, so investment also depends on the cash flow of the company.

currency board
A monetary authority that is required to maintain a fixed exchange ratio with respect to a foreign currency.

current account balance
Measured as the exports of goods and services from one country to the rest of the world, minus its imports of goods and services from the rest of the world, plus the net transfers that the country receives from abroad.

current expenditures (fiscal)
The sum of government spending, including wage payments, spending on goods and services, investment, and the payment of interest and transfers, such as welfare payments or housing subsidies.

current income (households)
The income that households receive in a certain period.

debt crisis
Massive increase in a government's debt beyond its expected tax revenues, possibly leading to default, and the events in the country occurring as a result of the default. An example is the Latin American debt crisis that developed in the early 1980s.

debt moratorium
A delay in the payment of debt obligations. It usually refers to a delay in the repayment of government debt..

deflation
Negative inflation; a drop in the general price level.

deglobalization
Reverse of globalization; consists in the disaggregation of countries in economic, technological, political, social, and cultural terms.

demand for labor
The amount of labor demanded by firms. Labor demand depends on the real wage, the capital stock, and technology. The higher the real wage, the lower is the quantity of labor demanded.

demand for money
The money that economic agents require to carry out their transactions or to store wealth. The amount depends on the agent's income level and the opportunity cost of holding money: the interest that would otherwise be earned is forgone.

depreciation (of capital)
A decrease in the economic value of the capital stock during a given period of time owing to the use of capital goods in production or unusable through obsolescence.

direct taxes
Taxes that apply directly to income or wealth.

discouraged worker effect
The phenomenon in which people unable to find work though looking for it, stop looking, and are no longer classified as unemployed. The discouraged worker effect can cause a fall in the unemployment rate. Compare with *additional worker effect*, which causes an increase in the unemployment rate.

division of labor
Segmentation of work tasks that allows efficiency improvements in the production process.

dollarization
An economy's adoption of the US dollar as its official currency. This results in a fixed exchange rate.

economic (or business) cycle
Short-term fluctuations in GDP around its long-term growth rate. When GDP rises, the economy is said to be in expansion phase, and when GDP falls, the economy is in a contraction phase. An economic cycle is measured from trough (lowest point) to trough.

economic growth
Sustained increase in the output of a country or region, usually measured as the increase in real GDP in per capita terms.

Economic and Monetary Union
A group of policies intended to bring together the economies of the member states of the European Union. EU countries use the same currency, the euro, and their monetary policies are decided by the European Central Bank.

economic policies
Set of rules that shape the economic system of a country, including fiscal, monetary, financial, and commercial policies.

environmental capital
The stock of natural resources and the quality of the environment of a country, with reference to such items as clean water and fertile soil.

equilibrium
State in which opposing forces are balanced, and in the absence of external influences, the values of the variables do not change. In economics, equilibrium is achieved when supply and demand are balanced.

expenditure taxes
Indirect taxes assessed on the purchase of goods and services.

exchange rate
Expression of the market value of one currency in terms of another currency.

external crisis
Economic crisis precipitated by the global economy. The main channel of transmission is the external sector of a country, but it can spread quickly to the other productive and financial sectors. .

external saving
Financial assets lent to a country by the rest of the world, which complement domestic savings. Positive external savings are equal to the current account deficit balance.

extreme poverty rate
A measure of the percentage of the population that lives on an income below the minimum needed to satisfy basic nutrition needs.

fiduciary money
Money whose value depends on people's trust that it stores value, despite not representing any amount of gold, silver, or other merchandise.

financial investment
Investments in financial instruments such as stocks, bonds, options, or investment funds.

fiscal balance
Difference between the revenues and the expenditures of the public sector. When the difference is positive (negative) there is a fiscal surplus (deficit).

fiscal (or government) budget
The total resources available to the public sector over a certain period of time.

fiscal deficit
An excess of government expenditure over government revenue. A fiscal deficit normally must be financed with public debt.

fixed exchange rate
Exchange rate scheme in which the exchange rate is pegged (or linked) to another currency, so a country's central bank undertakes to buy and sell foreign currency at the established rate.

flexible (or floating) exchange rate
Exchange rate scheme in which the exchange rate fluctuates freely according to market forces.

foreign currency reserves
International financial assets held by a country's central bank.

foreign direct investment
The purchase of controlling stakes of companies or assets by foreign investors.

GDP of full employment
Level of production that an economy reaches when the labor market is in equilibrium (everyone who is looking for a job can find one in a reasonable amount of time).

general government
Includes central government, local, and regional governments, as well as decentralized institutions such as national pension funds and state universities.

Gini coefficient
Measure of inequality that fluctuates between 0 and 1, where 0 indicates a totally equitable distribution and 1 corresponds to a scenario of complete inequality.

globalization
The economic integration of countries around the world, including the internationalization of production processes and the harmonization of economic institutions. Globalization has considerably increased the volume of trade and international capital flows.

gold standard
Monetary system massively adopted in the second half of the nineteenth century. Under this scheme, coins and notes have a value directly linked to gold, so they can be converted into gold according to an established parity.

government consumption
The aggregate amount of government spending on individual needs, such as the payment of public employees' salaries, and on community needs, such as goods and services for current consumption.

government investment
Aggregate amount of government investment, including various forms of capital expenditure, such as spending on the construction of public housing, roads, and ports.

government public spending
The aggregate amount of government consumption spending (salaries and purchases of goods and services), government investment, transfers to the private sector (welfare payments, subsidies), and interest on public debt.

Gresham's law
A monetary principle holding that "bad money drives out good." As originally conceived, the proposition was that when goods or coins of equal debt-paying value but unequal intrinsic value were both in circulation, the one of higher intrinsic value would be hoarded, leaving the one of lower intrinsic value in circulation. More broadly, superior value or practices have difficulty surviving.

gross domestic product
The total value of goods and services produced within the geographic limits of a country or region in a specific period of time.

gross investment
A business's total expenditure on capital goods—machinery, equipment, and plant.

gross national income
The value of the income generated by all the residents of a country in a specific period of time. It is equivalent to the gross national product plus net payments received by residents in foreign countries and some taxes not included in the valuation of production.

harmonization of economic institutions
The conscious decision of governments to make their economic institutions more compatible so that the rules of the game are increasingly similar throughout the world. Harmonization reduces the cost of doing business with other economies.

harmonized unemployment rate
Unemployment rate calculated by different countries using a similar measurement process so that the rate will be more comparable across countries.

human capital
The stock of skills and abilities that a worker has accumulated due to its investment in education and training. It determines the productive capacity of the labor force.

Human Development Index
An indicator created by the United Nations Development Program to achieve a more informative measure of economic well-being than per capita GDP. The index combines income per capita GDP with educational variables and the life expectancy rate in individual countries.

hysteresis
The continuation of effects after the causes of those effects have been removed. In economics, hysteresis describes the phenomenon whereby periods of high unemployment have permanent adverse effects on the labor market, increasing the natural rate of unemployment.

income effect
A fall (rise) in the price of a good that an individual consumes increases the purchasing power of the consumer affected, becoming richer (poorer) than before the price change affecting the individual's pattern of consumption. Compare with *substitution effect.*

income taxes
Direct taxes assessed on personal or corporate income.

indirect tax
Taxes that are not directly charged directly on individuals or businesses, but indirectly on the sale of goods and services (value-added tax) and other transactions.

Industrial Revolution
The deep technological transformation that began during the second half of the eighteenth century in England, then spread to Germany and the United States, changing the production process, with profound economic and social implications.

inflation
The percentage change in the general price level of an economy, usually measured by the variation in the consumer price index.

inflation expectations
Inflation rate anticipated by economic agents.

insolvency
Inability of an individual or entity to fully serve its debts using its current and future income.

interest on public debt
The cost (interest) that the government must pay every period to service its debt.

international capital flows
Movements of capital from one country to another, usually in the form of equity and debt instruments.

International Monetary Fund
An organization of 189 countries whose objectives are to encourage the development of global monetary cooperation, secure financial stability, facilitate international trade, promote high employment and sustainable economic growth, and reduce poverty around the world.

internationalization of production
Economic phenomenon in which capital or consumption goods are simultaneously national and foreign, with some parts produced in the country and other parts produced abroad.

intertemporal (decision)
Economic decision that relates present and future periods. A classic example is the decision about consumption: every penny that is not consumed today can be saved to be consumed later on.

inventory investment
Investment in raw materials, semifinished products, and finished goods that have not yet been sold and delivered to the final purchaser over a certain period. Compare with *fixed investment.*

investment
The part of production or income that, instead of being consumed, is used to accumulate capital and increase the productive capacity of the economy.

investment in fixed assets
Amount spent by companies on the plant, which is the physical structure that occupies a factory or a commercial office, and equipment, which corresponds mostly to machinery and vehicles.

investment in residential structures (residential investment)
Amount spent on the maintenance of existing housing and on new housing.

irreversibility (of investment)
Inability to undo an investment, or to undo it only at very high cost.

Keynesian animal spirits
A term coined by John Maynard Keynes to describe the relevance of emotions to investment decisions, rather than strict economic rationality.

labor force
The total number of people who are of working age and willing to work. The labor force comprises both employed and unemployed persons.

labor force surveys
Household surveys that are used to measure the performance of the labor market, including the unemployment rate and job creation rate, among other indicators.

labor market
A market bringing together demand for labor with offers of labor. Labor market equilibrium is reached when the real wage is such that the amount of labor demanded by firms equals the amount of labor offered by workers.

law of one price
Stipulation that in a free market, the price of an identical good or commodity traded anywhere should be the same when expressed in a common currency through the market exchange rate.

liberalization of capital flows
The reduction or elimination of controls on the free flow of capital between countries. The liberalization of capital flows is a main component of the globalization process.

liquidity constraint
Inability of some individuals or entities to borrow on the basis of their future income, as creditors assume these individuals will face difficulty in repaying the loan and do not have adequate credit guarantees.

lost decade (Latin America)
A decade of low GDP growth, rising population, and falling incomes owing to the debt crisis in the 1980s. At the end of the decade several Latin American countries had barely managed to recover to the levels of per capita GDP they had at the beginning of the decade.

long-term employment contracts
Wage contracts that last several years. The use of long-term employment contracts is common in countries that have gone through extended periods of high inflation.

macroeconomics
The branch of economics that studies the growth and fluctuations of a country or a region's economy from a broad perspective. It focuses on the aggregate variables of the economy, such as the level of production, unemployment rate, inflation rate, consumption, investment, trade, and the current account.

marginal productivity of labor
A measure of the increase in production resulting from increasing the labor input by a single unit; it is almost always positive.

means of exchange
A good or an asset that people accept as tradable for other goods or services, avoiding the need for barter. This is the main function of money.

monetary base
The total amount of currency that is either in general circulation in the hands of the public or held as commercial bank reserves.

monetary multiplier
Additional money generated by the actions of commercial banks for each dollar issued by the central bank (monetary base).

monetary policy
The specific macroeconomic policy that the central bank (or the monetary authority) uses to manage the money supply or the policy interest rate to maintain economic stability.

money market
A market bringing together the supply of and the demand for money. It determines the amount of money that people and companies hold.

money supply
The total value of money circulating in liquid instruments in a country at any time.

national savings
The sum of private savings and public sector savings. The national savings equals a country's income minus household consumption and government spending.

natural rate of unemployment
Unemployment rate that remains when the labor market (employers offering work and workers offering labor) is in equilibrium. The natural unemployment rate is also called the full employment rate of unemployment. It results from both frictional and structural factors and is part of the normal rotation existing in the labor market.

net creditor
An agent or entity with assets greater than liabilities (or debts).

net debtor
An agent or entity with liabilities (or debts) greater than assets.

net external assets position
The net stock of foreign assets that a country has over the rest of the world. When this position is positive (negative), it indicates that the country is a net creditor (debtor) relative to the rest of the world.

net investment
Measured as variation in the stock of capital between one period and another. Net investment is defined as gross investment minus the depreciation of capital stock.

net payments to domestic production factors
Correspond to the interests earned on net foreign assets, net profits on investment of residents abroad and net remittances sent to the country by nationals working abroad.

nominal GDP
The measure of GDP that indicates the value of goods and services at market prices.

nominal wage
Wage paid to a worker, expressed in current monetary units.

nonfinancial public sector
Aggregate of the general government and nonfinancial public enterprises.

nontariff barriers
Laws, regulations, or policies of a country that are not in the form of a tariff but have the effect of hindering imports. Some examples are quotas, previous deposits, or prohibitions against trading specific goods.

normative view
Approach that analyzes the economy based on what *should* happen. Compare *positive view*.

North American Free Trade Agreement (NAFTA)
An international trade agreement signed in January 1994 by Canada, the United States, and Mexico to reduce trade barriers between the three countries.

permanent income
Average of a person's current income and expected income in future periods; a kind of long-term average income.

political and economic institutions
Institutions key to the development of a country. Such institutions range from the judicial system and the political constitution to central bank autonomy and fiscal rules.

positive (negative) externality
The benefits (costs) of an economic activity that go beyond the direct effect on the economic agent that performs the activity and may have indirect benefits (costs) applicable to other agents. This is the case when social benefits are higher (lower) than private benefits.

positive view
Approach that analyzes the economy based on what *will* happen. Compare *normative view*.

potential level of output
The productive capacity of the economy, that is, the level of production that can be achieved when productive inputs are fully employed.

power of labor negotiation
The negotiating power of trade unions and other institutions responsible for setting wages.

precautionary savings
Tendency of people to save more when they face greater uncertainty about future income.

procyclical (fiscal)
Describes categories of public spending that tend to decrease in periods of recession periods and increase when the economy recovers, amplifying the economic cycle.

production function
Level of production that can be achieved with given levels of capital, labor, and technology.

property tax
Direct taxes assessed on the owners of properties such as land, housing, or buildings.

public debt
Debt owed by the public sector to domestic and foreign lenders. Public debt usually refers specifically to the debt owed by the central government.

purchasing power parity
A way to compare economic productivity and the standard of living between countries by setting equivalent prices, in the given currencies, for a standard basket of goods—the purchasing power of the currency.

quantitative easing
Unconventional monetary policy through which a central bank purchases public debt or other securities from the market in order to expand the money supply and stimulate the economy.

real GDP
Measure of the GDP that indicates the volume of goods and services produced. It is calculated as nominal GDP divided by the GDP deflator.

real wage
Wage expressed in terms of purchasing power. It is calculated by dividing the nominal wage by the price level.

recession
A general decline in economic activity. An economy is considered in recession after two consecutive quarters of negative GDP growth.

reserves requirement
Minimum amount of reserves that must be held by private banks in cash (or at the central bank), which restrains the amount of money a bank can lend to the public.

resource curse
The observed phenomenon that countries reliant on abundant natural resources seem to grow less economically than resource-scarce economies.

sacrifice coefficient

The cost in terms of unemployment of each percentage point by which inflation is reduced. It is measured by the excess of unemployment accumulated above its equilibrium level (the *natural* rate), divided by the reduction of inflation, during a stabilization program.

self-fulfilling prophecy

A belief that, if widely held and subsequently acted upon, is realized. For example, if everyone thinks there will be a recession, nobody invests, and indeed, the recession eventually arrives.

sovereign loans

Debt issued by a national government.

specialization

Restriction of workers' activities to a relatively narrow range. Specialization is expected to increase economic efficiency and growth.

speculative attack

Massive exchange of national money for foreign currency in the expectation of a collapse of a managed exchange rate scheme. A speculative attack depletes the reserves of the central bank and precipitates a large depreciation of the currency.

stock of capital

The physical capital that is used in the production process of a firm. Capital stock includes machinery, buildings, transportation, and office supplies, among other physical assets. The aggregate capital stock of an economy determines its productive capacity.

storage of value

The ability of money to maintain its power to purchase goods and services over time. Stored value can be reduced under conditions of high inflation or hyperinflation.

structural characteristics

Geographic elements such as location, climate, or access to the sea that affect the costs of trade, labor productivity, and returns on agriculture, among other economic variables.

structural balance rule
Rule specifying that the government must fix fiscal expenditures in a way that guarantees a certain structural deficit (or surplus) as a specific percentage of GDP. This provides an automatic stabilization mechanism: a moderate fiscal deficit is allowed in recessions, while in booms, the government commits to a surplus.

structural fiscal balance
The fiscal balance that would exist if the economy were at its potential level of overall output. The influence of the economic cycle is excluded.

subprime mortgage crisis
Economic crisis detonated in the United States in 2008 that quickly spread to the rest of the world. The crisis was caused by credit deterioration following the housing bubble, and in particular by the expansion of high-risk (subprime) mortgages.

substitution effect
A fall (rise) in the price of a good consumed by an individual (everything else held constant) makes that good relatively cheaper (more expensive) than other goods, so the consumer will try to consume more (less) of the good.

systemic (financial) risk
Risk that affects the entire financial system rather than simply the failure of individual parts of the system. Systemic risk could trigger severe instability or a collapse of the entire financial sector.

tariffs
Levies assessed on imported goods and services. Tariffs commonly seek to protect domestic industry by increasing the prices of foreign products.

technological progress
The invention and adoption of new technologies, resulting in the creation of new products, as well as the ability to produce at lower cost. Technological progress is one of the most important drivers of economic growth.

terms of trade
Economic variable that expresses the price of exports in terms of imports. It shows how expensive the exports of a country are with respect to the value of the goods that are imported.

total factor productivity
The component of economic growth that is not explained by an increase in production inputs (capital and labor). Total factor productivity is interpreted as the fraction of economic growth attributable to technological progress.

trade balance
Difference between the exports and imports of a country (net exports). When the difference is positive (negative) there is a trade surplus (deficit).

transfers to the private sector
Government spending directed to the private sector. It includes retirement pensions, unemployment insurance, war veterans' benefits, and health benefits among many other benefits.

Treaty of Maastricht
Agreement signed by the members of the European Union in 1991 to achieve greater convergence in economic policies in order to facilitate the establishment of a common monetary policy.

Treaty of Rome
Agreement signed in 1957 by Belgium, France, Italy, Luxembourg, the Netherlands, and West Germany to create the European Economic Community and so begin the process of European unification.

underemployment
Employment in activities that require less skill than the incumbent has, or for fewer hours than the incumbent wants to work.

unemployment rate
Percentage of the labor force that is actively searching for a job without finding one.

unilateral transfers
Donations received from other nations that are posted to the current account of the recipient nation's balance of payments.

unit of account
Standardized unit by which the value of something is measured in a specific currency. The ability of money to express the prices of all goods in a single denomination means only a single price for each good is needed for transactions to occur.

urbanization
Concentration of the population in relatively large and dense settlements.

wage indexation
Automatic adjustment of nominal wages based on past inflation. This practice is common in countries that have gone through long periods of high inflation.

Washington Consensus
Set of policy recommendations made after the debt crisis of the 1980s that sought to prevent future crises in developing countries. It was agreed that granting loans to developing countries would be conditional on their certain goals or policy prescriptions, to include economic liberalization, stabilization, and trade openness policies.

work supply
Relationship between the amount of labor offered by households and the real wage, given a certain level of capital and technology. The higher the real wage, the larger the quantity of labor offered.

World Bank
International economic institution with 189 member countries, founded in 1944 at the Bretton Woods Conference. As a global partnership, the World Bank is committed to reducing poverty, supporting economic growth, and ensuring sustainable grains in the quality of people's lives.

World Happiness Index
Indicator calculated by the World Economic Forum as a measure of overall well-being in a country. The index is constructed according to subjective indicators obtained from the direct responses of people and is a complement to welfare measures based on hard economic data.

World Trade Organization
International organization with 164 member countries that was founded in 1995. It seeks to open up trade around the world by easing the negotiation of trade agreements, reducing the obstacles to international trade, and ensuring a level playing field for all countries.

BIBLIOGRAPHY

Alesina, Alberto, and Lawrence Summers. "Central Bank Independence and Macroeconomic Performance: Some Comparative Evidence." *Journal of Money, Credit and Banking* (e-journal) 25, no. 2 (1993): 151–162.

Armendáriz, Beatriz, and Felipe Larraín B. *The Economics of Contemporary Latin America.* Cambridge, MA: MIT Press, 2017.

Arnone, Marco, Bernard J. Laurens, Jean-François Segalotto, and Martin Sommer. "Central Bank Autonomy: Lessons from Global Trends." *IMF Staff Papers* 56, no. 2 (2009): 263–296.

Bank of Mexico (Banco de México). http:www.banxico.org.mx.

Boschini, A. D., J. Pettersson, and J.Roine. "Resource Curse or Not: A Question of Appropriability." *Scandinavian Journal of Economics* 109, no. 3 (2007): 593–617.

Bureau of Economic Analysis. http:www.bea.gov.

Bureau of Labor Statistics. http:www.bls.gov.

Busse, Matthias. "Tariffs, Transport Costs and the WTO Doha Round: The Case of Developing Countries." *Journal of International Law and Trade Policy* 4, no. 1 (2003): 24.

Central Bank of Chile (Banco Central de Chile). http:www.bcentral.cl.

Dollar, David, and Aart Kraay. "Foreign Trade, Growth and Poverty." *Finance and Development* 38, no. 3 (2001): 30.

European Central Bank. 2017. Statistical Data Warehouse (databases). Brussels: European Central Bank Eurosystem, 2017. http://sdw.ecb.europa.eu.

Executive Office of the President's Council of Economic Advisers. *Economic Report of the President,* figure B-42, 64. Washington, DC: US Government Printing Office, 1998.

Federal Reserve Bank of St. Louis. FRED Economic Data (databases). https://fred.stlouisfed.org.

Government of Spain. Real Decreto-Ley 3/2012. *Boletín Oficial del Estado,* February 10, 2012. https://www.boe.es/boe/dias/2012/02/11/pdfs/BOE-A -2012-2076.pdf.

Helliwell, J., E. Layard, and J. Sachs. *World Happiness Report 2018*. New York: Sustainable Development Solutions Network, 2018.

International Monetary Fund. "Exchange Rate and International Reserves in Mexico, 1994–1995." *International Financial Statistics*. Washington, DC: IMF, 1999. CD-ROM.

International Monetary Fund. Government Finance Statistics (databases). Washington, DC: IMF. https://data.imf.org.

International Monetary Fund. *International Financial Statistics*. http://data.imf.org.

International Monetary Fund. *Macroeconomic and Financial Data: Balance of Payments and International Investment Position Statistics*. Washington, DC: IMF, 2018. http://data.imf.org.

International Monetary Fund. *Macroeconomic and Financial Data: Government Finance Statistics*. Washington, DC: IMF, 2018. http://data.imf.org.

International Monetary Fund. *World Economic Outlook, April 2018*. Washington, DC: IMF, 2018. https://www.imf.org/external/pubs/ft/weo/2016/02/weodata/index.aspx.

Kennedy, Robert F. "Speech at the University of Kansas, March 18, 1968." https://www.jfklibrary.org/learn/about-jfk/the-kennedy-family/robert-f-kennedy/robert-f-kennedy-speeches/remarks-at-the-university-of-kansas-march-18-1968.

Keynes, John Maynard. *The General Theory of Employment, Interest and Money*. London: Macmillan, 1936.

Lakner, Christoph, and Branko Milanovic. "Global Income Distribution: From the Fall of the Berlin Wall to the Great Recession." Policy Research Working Paper no. WPS 6719. New York: World Bank Group, 2013.

Larraín B., Felipe. "Public Sector Behavior in a Highly Indebted Country: The Contrasting Chilean Experience." In *The Public Sector and the Latin American Crisis*, edited by Felipe Larraín B. and Marcelo Selowsky. San Francisco: ICS Press, 1991.

Larraín, Felipe, and Oscar Perelló. "Resource Windfalls and Public Sector Employment: Evidence from Municipalities in Chile." *Economia* 19, no. 2 (2019): 127–167.

Larraín B., Felipe, and Jeffrey D. Sachs. *Macroeconomics in the Global Economy.* 3rd ed. Santiago: Pearson Educación de Chile, 2013.

Maddison, Angus. *Phases of Capitalist Development.* Oxford: Oxford University Press, 1982.

Maddison Project. Maddison Project Database. http://www.ggdc.net/maddison/maddison-project/home.htm.

Malthus, Thomas. "First Essay on Population 1798." London: Macmillan, [1798] 1996, 139. Cited in Angus Maddison, *Phases of Capitalist Development.* Oxford: Oxford University Press, 1982, 9.

Milanovic, Branko. *Global Inequality.* Cambridge, MA: Harvard University Press, 2016.

Montevideo-Oxford Latin American Economic History Database (MOxLAD). https://libraries.usc.edu/databases/montevideo-oxford-latin-american-economic-history-database-moxlad.

National Institute of Statistics and Censuses of the Argentine Republic (INDEC). www.indec.gov.ar.

National Institute of Statistics (Instituto Nacional de Estadística España). http:www.ine.es.

National Institute of Statistics (Instituto Nacional de Estadísticas Chile). http:www.ine.cl.

Nissanke, Machiki, and Erik Thorbecke. 2006. "Channels and Policy Debate in the Globalization-Inequality-Poverty Nexus." Discussion Paper 2005/008, 23. Helsinki: UNU-WIDER, 2005.

Organisation for Economic Co-operation and Development. Data (databases). Paris: OECD. https://data.oecd.org.

Paredes, Carlos. "The Behavior of the Public Sector in Peru: A Macroeconomic Approach." In Larraín B. and Selowsky, *The Public Sector and the Latin American Crisis.* San Francisco: ICS Press, 1991.

Rodrik, Dani. *The Globalization Paradox: Democracy and the Future of the World Economy.* New York: W. W. Norton, 2010.

Roser, Max, and Ortiz-Ospina, Esteban. "Global Extreme Poverty." OurWorldinData.org, first published in 2013; last substantive revision March 27, 2017. https://ourworldindata.org/extreme-poverty.

Sachs, J. D., and A. M. Warner. "The Curse of Natural Resources." *European Economic Review* 45, nos. 4–6 (2001): 827–838.

Sala-i-Martin, Xavier. "The World Distribution of Income: Falling Poverty and … Convergence, Period." *Quarterly Journal of Economics* 121, no. 2 (2006): 351–397.

Sala-i-Martin, Xavier. "Consequences of BREXIT." Author's blog, June 25, 2016. http://salaimartin.com/randomthoughts/item/767-las-consecuencias -del-brexit.html#.

Soros, George. *On Globalization.* New York: Public Affairs, 2002.

Stiglitz, Joseph. *Globalization and Its Discontents.* New York: W. W. Norton, 2002.

Stiglitz, Joseph. *Making Globalization Work.* New York: W. W. Norton, 2006.

Stiglitz, Joseph E., and José Antonio Ocamp, eds. *Capital Market Liberalization and Development.* Oxford: Oxford University Press, 2008.

United Nations Conference on Trade and Development. *World Investment Report 2018.* New York and Geneva: United Nations, 2018. https://unctad.org/ en/PublicationsLibrary/wir2018_en.pdf.

United States Census Bureau. www.census.gov.

University of Michigan. *Surveys of Consumers,* 2017. http://www.sca.isr.umich .edu.

Van der Ploeg, Frederick. "Natural Resources: Curse or Blessing?" *Journal of Economic Literature* 49, no. 2 (2011): 366–420.

World Bank. *Doing Business.* Washington, DC: World Bank. http://www.doing business.org.

World Bank. *The East Asian Miracle: Economic Growth and Public Policy.* Washington, DC: World Bank, 1993.

World Bank. *World Development Indicators.* Washington, DC: World Bank, 2018. http://databank.worldbank.org/data/reports.aspx?source=world-develop ment-indicators.

World Economic Forum. *World Happiness Report 2018.* https://worldhappiness .report/ed/2018.

FURTHER READING

Acemoglu, Daron, and James A. Robinson. *Why Nations Fail: The Origins of Power, Prosperity, and Poverty*. Reprint. New York: Crown/Currency, 2013.

Eichengreen, Barry. *The Populist Temptation: Economic Grievance and Political Reaction in the Modern Era*. Oxford: Oxford University Press, 2018.

Larraín, Felipe, and Jeffrey Sachs. *Macroeconomics in the Global Economy*. New York: Prentice Hall, 1993.

Rajan, Raghuram. *How Markets and the State Leave the Community Behind*. New York: Penguin Random House, 2019.

Rodrik, Dani. *Straight Talk on Trade: Ideas for a Sane World Economy*. Princeton, NJ: Princeton University Press, 2017.

Roubini, Nouriel, and Stephen Mihm. *Crisis Economics: A Crash Course in the Future of Finance*. New York: Penguin, 2010.

Spence, Michael. *The Next Convergence: The Future of Economic Growth in a Multispeed World*. New York: Farrar, Straus and Giroux, 2011.

Stiglitz, Joseph, 2017. *Globalization and Its Discontents Revisited: Anti-Globalization in the Era of Trump*. New York: W. W. Norton, 2017.

INDEX

The MIT Press Essential Knowledge Series

FELIPE LARRAÍN B. is Professor of Economics at Catholic University of Chile, was Director of the Latin American Center of Economics and Social Policies (CLAPES UC), and was Finance Minister of Chile twice, from 2010 to 2014 and from 2018 to 2019. The coauthor (with Jeffrey D. Sachs) of *Macroeconomics in the Global Economy* and (with Beatriz Armendáriz) of *The Economics of Contemporary Latin America* (MIT Press), he has published fifteen books and more than 120 scholarly articles. He has been named Finance Minister of the Year for Latin America and the Americas several times.

The MIT Press Essential Knowledge Series

A complete list of the titles in this series appears at the back of this book.

MACROECONOMICS